Early Days at the Mission
San Juan Bautista

By ISAAC L. MYLAR

A narrative of incidents connected with the
days when California was young

PUBLISHED BY
EVENING PAJARONIAN
WATSONVILLE, CALIFORNIA
1929

PUBLISHED 1985 BY
PANORAMA WEST BOOKS
In Cooperation With
SAN JUAN BAUTISTA STATE PARK
VOLUNTEER ASSOCIATION

Printed in the United States of America

Introduction

SAAC L. MYLAR'S reminiscenes of persons, places, and events in and around San Juan Bautista, principally between 1855 and 1880, are among the relatively few available accounts of the "City of History" in the early years of its American period. For this reason, the San Juan Bautista Historical Society decided in the summer of 1970 to reissue the out-of-print publication as a service to the increasing thousands who are interested in the history of California in general and of San Juan in particular.

While the text of Mr. Mylar's narrative remains unchanged, the new volume has been provided with a revised table of contents, appropriate new pictures from the Society's historical files, and an appendix designed to correct significant errors resulting from faulty transcription or the occasional quirk of a well-tested memory, and also to present a limited amount of related and possibly elusive material.

The story of the Mylar family is a survey-in-miniature of the whole Westward movement. Isaac Mylar's grandparents, James and Henrietta Jette) Mylar, were born, respectively, in South Carolina and Virginia; his parents, Israel and Mary (Walters) Mylar, in Kentucky and Ohio; and his own generation in Illinois, Missouri, and California.

Dorothy Flint
San Juan Bautista Historical Society
1970

Foreword

I TAKE this method of stating that I make no pretensions to being a writer and would not have undertaken this task had I not been urged to do so by my friends and acquaintances. I have set down here faithfully, as memory serves me, many incidents of my life in San Juan from 1855 until 1880. After that date (1880) there are many living who, possibly, could relate better than I the incidents connected with San Juan up to the present time. I have told my story briefly and simply. If I have made mistakes in these memoirs, I trust that I may be pardoned, for it is rather difficult to look back and remember things correctly for seventy or seventy-five years. I hope that these little incidents that I have set down will prove of interest not only to the descendants of those grand old pioneers that stood by San Juan from the beginning to the present time, but that everyone may enjoy its reading as much as I have enjoyed reciting it to my friend, Jas. G. Piratsky, Editor of the Evening Pajaronian, Watsonville, California.

I send my little message out with keen enjoyment, for its telling brought back to me the many happy days I spent in San Juan Bautista.

I have not, in my "Recollections," attempted to give any history of the Mission of San Juan Bautista. I feel that I would not be able for the task, so leave that pleasant duty to someone better fitted than my humble self.

ISAAC L. MYLAR.

I desire to add to the above that I have never engaged in a more pleasant task than in listening to Mr. Isaac Mylar's reminiscences connected with the Mission San Juan Bautista, San Benito county. Mr. Mylar told his story tersely and so much to the point that I felt that I would be doing him an injustice if I endeavored to clothe his simply told story with flowery language or rhetorical flights.

A matter of wonderment too, is Mr. Mylar's remarkable memory. Although now eighty years of age he relates incidents connected with his boyhood, in San Juan, with a clearness that is certainly remarkable for a man of his age.

JAS. G. PIRATSKY.

MISSION SAN JUAN BAUTISTA CIRCA 1860

			Page
Chapter	I	Arrival in California and San Juan	13
Chapter	II	Acquaintance With the Mission	19
Chapter	III	Early Schools and Teachers	27
Chapter	IV	Metropolis on El Camino Real	35
Chapter	V	A Land Grant and Its Settlers	39,
Chapter	VI	Along the Roads to San Juan	47
Chapter	VII	Orientation on Third Street	51
Chapter	VIII	More Streets and Buildings	61
Chapter	IX	Exploring First and Second Streets	69
Chapter	X	The Mission Acres and Their Environment	79
Chapter	XI	Lawlessness and Organized Banditry	89
Chapter	XII	"Land of Milk and Honey"	97
Chapter	XIII	Providing, Preparing and Conserving Food	103
Chapter	XIV	Of Neighboring Sawmills and Gristmills	107
Chapter	XV	Professional Men and Local Officials	111
Chapter	XVI	San Juan in Civil War Years	117
Chapter	XVII	Roads, Indian Settlements, and a Grove	121
Chapter	XVIII	Stagecoach Days at San Juan	127
Chapter	XIX	Occasions for Gala Celebrations	131
Chapter	XX	After a Flood, a Long Drought	137
Chapter	XXI	Reactions to Disaster and Loss	143
Chapter	XXII	Smallpox and a Great Earthquake	147
Chapter	XXIII	Beginnings of the Town of Hollister	151
Chapter	XXIV	Division of Monterey County	157
Chapter	XXV	Newspapers for a New Era	163
Chapter	XXVI	Weathering Another Dry Year	167
Chapter	XXVII	Mark Regan, Stage Driver and Raconteur	173
Chapter	XXVIII	A Philanthropist and His Neighbors	179
Chapter	XXIX	From Sheep Dip to Cement Plant	185
		Notes and References	196
		Index	199

ARCHED CORRIDOR OF MISSION SAN JUAN BAUTISTA

San Juan Bautista Mission

UT LITTLE was known of the interior of California prior to the commencement of the Mission era, or 1769, although various navigators had sailed along the California coast during the period intervening between the time of its discovery by Cabrillo in 1642, and the advent of the Franciscan missionaries.

The Indians had roamed through the mountains and plains of this western coast for unknown ages, living a degraded life, but little above the level of that of the wild animals indigenous to this region. Of their origin or history there is no record. Aside from the story of the rocks, and the vague lessons taught by the topography of the country, we know absolutely nothing of Alta California prior to 1642, nor, indeed, very little until the latter part of the eighteenth century. The historical period, therefore, may be said to commence with the founding of the Missions.

During Father Junipero Serra's noble administration nine Missions had been founded in Alta or Upper California. These Missions had gathered many Indians into their fold, or had brought them under their control, and they had also acquired considerable wealth in the form of cattle, horses, sheep and other useful animals, and grain, etc.

In November, 1795, Friar Danti and Lieutenant Sal and party set out from Monterey to explore the San Benito valley, and they found one site on the San Benito river and the other near the site of the present town of Gilroy. President Lasuen reported these to Governor Borica, who embodied the same in his reports to the Viceroy. As two sites had been recommended for the Mission between San Carlos and Santa Clara, a further examination was ordered, and a site on the San Benito river was chosen.

Here, on St. John's day, June 24th, 1797, was founded the Mission San Juan Bautista (St. John the Baptist), so named to distinguish it from the Mission already established, of San Juan Capistrano, which was named after an entirely different person-age or saint.

A few years after, or on the 13th of June, 1803, the corner stone of the church building was laid. Among the names of the persons who took part in the ceremonies of laying the corner stone of this church, over 100 years ago, were Padre Viader, conductor of ceremonies, Jose de la Guerra, Pardino and Captain Font and Surgeon Morelas. The record of the proceedings and a few coins were deposited in the corner stone. An image of the patron saint of the Mission, St. John the Baptist, was placed on the high altar in 1809, and on the 25th of June, 1812, the church was dedicated, the records of the Missions noting the contemporary facts to Fernando the VII and others.

Probably the buildings, including the church warehouses, etc., as they exist at the present day, afford a fair idea of the Mission establishment as it appeared during the early part of the century, less the busy and numerous neophyte actors, and the missionary fathers under whom they labored. These buildings, of course, show the effect of time and action of the elements; nevertheless, they are still in a fair state of preservation, and they show plainly, even to this day, that their designers and builders were wise managers in temporal affairs.

The San Juan church was built of adobe and slack-burnt bricks—the latter being 12 by 8 inches and two inches thick; and being baked in a slow fire, were very durable. The plan of the building was in the form of a cross, being 140 feet long, 30 feet wide, and 40 feet to the ceiling, with a tile roofing. There were three altars, the principal one dedicated to St. John the Baptist, with a life-size statue of this titular saint at the end of the nave of the church, and an altar on each side of the transept. The walls are four feet thick, braced with brick abutment outside over 20 feet long, and plastered with lime mortar. The church formerly had a chime of nine very fine-toned bells, cast in Peru, only one of which now remains in the building.

The Mission of San Juan Bautista owned in 1820 over 40,000 head of cattle, nearly 1,400 tame horses and about 70,000 head of sheep. Indians, under the control of the Mission, employed more than 300 yoke of work oxen in carrying on extensive farming operations.

In 1813 and again in 1828 the Spanish Cortez decreed the secularization of Missions in all Spanish colonies. The Mexican congress, August 17th, 1833, passed a secularization law which was effectually enforced within two or three years thereafter.— [The foregoing history is taken from "The Memorial History of the Coast Counties of Central California."]

CASTRO ADOBE—1841

CHAPTER 1

The author's arrival in California—The stay at Vallecitos—
Removal to Shaw's Flat—Family treks south—After
reaching the Salinas river returns to San Juan.

Y PARENTS crossed the plains in a covered wagon, drawn by three yoke of oxen, in 1852. We arrived in California about the first of October of that year. It took five months to make the trip. There were about sixty immigrants in the train. The trip across the country was uneventful, devoid of any excitement except that one of the immigrants died of cholera. Luckily, the disease did not spread among the rest of the immigrants, and we were spared the usual horror that accompanies an epidemic of that nature.

We crossed the Sierras and, descending into California, my parents stopped at Vallecitos, Calaveras county, after passing through Placerville (at that time known as "Hangtown"). "Hangtown," as it was then known, was the abiding place of Studebaker; in after years, the millionaire manufacturer of the Studebaker wagons and buggies, and finally the celebrated Studebaker automobile. Studebaker, while living in Placerville, conducted a blacksmith shop and made a large sum of money constructing wheel-barrows as a side line. These wheel-barrows were purchased by miners to be used in mining operations.

At the time that my parents stopped at Vallecitos, I was nearly five years of age. Our stay in Vallecitos was marked by two incidents which still stand out clearly in my mind. One was the serious illness of my dear mother who fell quite ill after the long journey across the plains. The other incident was my embarking in the poultry-raising business.

My father showed me how to look in the crevices of the bedrock for gold. I would look along the little ravines close to the cabin where we lived and would find small nuggets wedged in these crevices. Perhaps there had been dozens who had gone over the same ground and picked up the larger pieces. Those I got ranged from five to fifty cents in value. One weighed two dollars and fifty cents. I would take these and put them in a little gourd at the head of my mother's bed. One of the neighboring miners had a hen and five small chicks and I greatly coveted them. He asked ten dollars for the lot; mother said, "Father will weigh your gold at noon and if you have enough you can buy them." When I poured it on the scales father laughed and said, "You're a pretty good miner." I had nearly fifteen dollars. He weighed out enough for ten dollars, (most of the miners had gold scales in those days), and I bought the hen and chicks. Father fixed up a coop back of the cabin for the hen and her chicks. I was up early the next morning to attend to my chickens, but, great grief, a fox had taken the lot. It was a hard blow for me.

I will always remember how I went broke in the chicken business.

After stopping a short time at Vallecitos my parents moved to Shaw's Flat, Tuolumne county—between Sonora and Columbia, on the "Mother Lode."

Here my sister was born on the side of Table Mountain, on Feb. 22, 1855. She afterwards married Wm. Allyn and is now residing in Oakland.

For nearly three years my father mined, with varying success, at Shaw's Flat. Looking back over that period I recall that at the same time that my father was mining there, so was a hard-working energetic young miner known as Jim Fair, afterwards Senator James Fair; the man who built the Fair fortune and often boasted that he "never would be traced by the quarters that he dropped!" At the time when Fair and my father were mining there they were engaged in working on a channel that was about a rod wide and some sixteen to eighteen feet deep. This channel ran into Table Mountain, the mountain afterwards celebrated by Mark Twain in his story, "The Jumping Frog of Calaveras," when Mark was living with Steve Gillis, on the "Mother Lode." Both Fair and my father owned separate claims although they were working on the same channel. Under the law a claim was limited to one hundred feet in length. Right above my father's claim was another claim operated by a man by the name of Caldwell. Out of his one hundred feet he took $75,000 worth of gold. The gravel from Caldwell's mine was hoisted to the surface by means of a windlass and then run through a Long Tom. I remember, one night, seeing them weigh the day's receipts and they had thirteen pounds of gold. The magnitude of this take may be judged from the fact that the gold taken from Table Mountain averaged nearly pure gold, and, if taken to the mint, commanded $19.50 per ounce, making the "take" for the day about $3,000. On my father's claim it averaged about $5,000 to the hundred feet but Caldwell struck a rich rough ledge—in fact everyone on the channel made big money.

During our stay there I attended a public school that was located at Springfield, between Shaw's Flat and Columbia. Columbia, Tuolumne county, at that time, contained a population of something like 15,000 souls. Its importance may be judged from the fact that it reached for the location of the state capital at one time, and its chances were considered good. It is now one of the "Ghost Cities" of the "Mother Lode" and contains about twenty inhabitants.

After mining at Shaw's Flat my parents moved south through Livermore Pass and entering upon "El Camino Real" (The King's Highway) proceeded through, what was then known as the Mission of San Jose, in Alameda County, and traveling southward through San Jose, past the Mission of Santa Clara. San Jose, then, was a mere hamlet of no importance whatever. Wending our way southward my parents passed through the Mission San Juan Bautista and crossed over San Juan hill—there was no grade[1] there at that time, and descended into what was then known as the "Salinas plains"—

now called the Salinas Valley. The Salinas Valley, at that time, was covered with a wild growth of timber and heavy crops of mustard and tenanted by droves of antelope and other game.

There were, even at that early date, a few houses at Natividad, where had occurred the celebrated "Battle of Natividad" between the Mexicans and gringos.

"The Battle of Natividad," which occurred in December, 1846, was between a detachment of men commanded by a Captain Foster and a force sent after them by Governor Pico from Monterey. Foster's detachment were United States soldiers and were engaged in bringing a band of horses from the North to Los Angeles. Pico's detachment was sent to not only stop the soldiers from passing through, but to capture the horses. The horses were run into a narrow canyon somewhere, I think, over on the Alisal. The scrimmage was short and sanguinary as Captain Foster was killed as were also eleven of his men. I don't know how many were killed on the Mexican side but undoubtedly they paid dearly for 'their temerity in attacking the Americans. It was said afterwards that this engagement was the only fight ever known in which the Mexicans got the best of the Americans. However, the Mexicans did not succeed in their attempt to capture the band of horses.

We camped on the bank of the Salinas river that afternoon and awaited the return of my father, who, struck by the business activity and picturesque location of San Juan, had retraced his steps to that town. Finding some families, who were anxious to return to Carson, Nevada, he bought one hundred and sixty acres which they had taken up. This land was located about one mile south of town, adjoining the John Breen tract. The land bought was well fenced and contained a two-story frame structure which had been erected in 1852. The house was well built and there was not a piece of sawed wood in it, all the lumber being split stuff, even to the floor, and planed by hand.

As soon as my father consummated this transaction our family traveled back to San Juan. My mother was delighted with the location of our new home and said that she never wanted to leave it. She never did. She lived there eleven years before she died.

The loss of my mother was a great misfortune to all of us, and we grieved over her passing away for a long time. To me, she embodied all that was charming, beautiful and lovable. My father, who was inclined to travel greatly—in fact was afflicted with the wanderlust, missed her sorely, and for a time it seemed as though our home might be broken up if our father took to the road again in search of fresh fields and pastures new.

OLD MISSION BELLS CIRCA 1865

CHAPTER II

The Mission Bells that filled the vale with melody—Secularization of the Missions by the Mexican Government—The little Mission cemetery wherein thousands were buried

---

T SAN JUAN, in the shadow of the old mission church—built there in 1797, I grew to manhood. The Angelus bells rang out, sending their silvery tones over the peaceful valley each morning, noon and evening, and I remember we would set our watches by the mission bells. It was solar time that was given to us. The Padres, or their assistants, took the time by a large sun-dial that was in the mission yard. The bells, also, rang out at eight o'clock, each evening, serving as a notice for everyone to retire for the night; this latter signal was intended for the Indians, whose welfare was looked after closely by the mission fathers. The six o'clock Angelus bell was a notification for them to prepare and eat their evening meal. The eight o'clock bell was for them to retire, as they were not allowed to roam around at night. When we came to San Juan the mission boasted of three bells attached to a long beam which was supported about ten feet from the ground by two immense posts, sunk in the ground, and these bells were located about thirty feet from the front of the church door. The stroke was made by a piece of rawhide being attached to each clapper (or bell tongue). They were a fine set of bells; at times, according to the temperature, silvery and then apparently golden in tone. They could be heard from six to seven miles—yes, even over to the sheep ranch owned by Mr. Hollister, now the site of the flourishing county seat of San Benito county. Ah! many a time those silvery-sounding bells, which linger yet in memory's recollection, warned me to hurry home for meals. In due time, by some means or another, two of these beautiful bells were cracked and the mission fathers had them recast. I do not know where the fathers sent them to be recast; probably in Mexico. On their return the bells were encased in a belfry, which was located in the side of the church. Probably the old bells resented this belfry, for, somehow or another, they never again gave forth the silvery tones that were so charming in the days gone by. It was alleged that the old bells contained a large portion of silver which made them give forth the silvery tones in the past and that whoever recast them took away from the molten metal a large proportion of the silver—in fact, stole it—and replaced the silver with some other metal. Be that as it may, to my mind, the bells never again were the same. Superstition alleged that the bells felt ill at ease in this belfry, that they were not the same in tone—apparently out of tune in their new environment.

In 1845 San Juan was declared a pueblo by Governor Pico, and it was either in that year or the following year, if I remember aright, that the Mexican government secularized the missions.[2] In other words, their wealth, growth and prosperity excited the cupidity and avarice of the officials, then ruling Mexico, and they took from the missions, the greater portion of their holdings, in fact, some of the missions' rich land-holdings were sold to covetous purchasers. It was a dreadful blow to the missions and also to the Indians who had been so carefully cared for by the mission fathers. It was a blow from which the missions never recovered.

When the secularization of the missions by the Mexican government took place the lands of the various missions were sold to different buyers. Here are some of the sales that were made: the lands belonging to the Mission San Diego were sold to Santiago Arguello, June 8, 1846; those belonging to San Luis Rey sold to Antonio Cot and Andreas Pico, May, 1846; San Juan Capistrano, was left a pueblo and the remainder of the land sold to John Foster and Jas. McKinley, December, 1845; San Gabriel Mission was sold to John Workman and Hugo Reid, June, 1846; San Fernando Mission was sold to Juan Celis, June, 1846; San Buena Ventura was sold to Joseph Anzar; La Purissima was sold to John Temple, Dec., 1845; Soledad, house and garden to Soberanos, January, 1846.

The missions San Juan Bautista, San Juan Capistrano, San Francisco and Carmel were named as pueblos. There is no record of any of the lands being taken away from these pueblo missions and sold by Governor Pico, under whose regime all these sales were consummated.

At the time that we came to San Juan a large portion of the holdings of the San Juan Mission had passed from the control of the mission fathers, how much I do not know; I was too young, at that time, to realize the grave injustice that had been done to the missions and Indians, but I remember that the Mission San Juan Bautista had a magnificent orchard on the bottom-land adjoining our place. This orchard, which embraced thirty-six acres, was planted to grapes and pears and there was in it, I remember, one apple and one peach tree also several large olive trees that yielded fine crops of olives. This orchard, instead of being fenced in, was surrounded by a ditch some ten to twelve feet deep and about five feet wide, which was intended to keep cattle out and was, for that purpose, effectual. Traces of this ditch still can be seen. There was another orchard of ten acres down the hill to the flat, which was planted to pears and some apples. This orchard was surrounded by a deep ditch. There were, in this orchard, pear trees one hundred years old; great big, massive trees, bearing luscious pears. Some of these trees were sixty to seventy feet high. I remember them well, for often did I climb over the brush fence to pick the pears off the ground and eat until I could eat no more.

Back of the mission church, today there is an enclosed place which was the original burial ground connected with the mission. At the present time it possesses some of the finest olive trees on the Pacific coast. In this small enclosure are buried a large number of Indians, some say up into the thousands. An explanation of this may be found in the fact that this small enclosed space was the only consecrated ground connected with the mission, and was originally consecrated by one of the bishops, who came from Mexico.   As the little space filled it was found impossible to get another bishop to come from Mexico and it was against the rules of the church to be buried outside of consecrated ground.   Consequently, the little enclosure today is packed with the bones of a multitude of Indian adherents of the Catholic church.   I remember seeing them bury some of those Indians.   They would dig the grave and in digging the grave they found it necessary to remove the bones of some former Indian who was buried close by the grave or possibly interred in the grave.   These bones were tenderly and reverently resurrected and placed alongside the new grave and then, when the coffin or body was laid in its earthen receptacle, the bones were carefully replaced alongside the person buried.   Nowadays, of course, imagination has run riot over early episodes in San Juan and I have heard it asserted, as a fact, that upwards of four to six thousand bodies were buried in that small enclosure. I cannot say that this is true.   I do not know; but I know that a great many bodies were interred there.

The little frame school house that I attended when a boy is still standing on its original site near the cemetery on the road to "The Rocks."   Speaking of the cemetery, reminds me that in the early days, Manuel Larios was the owner of what was then known as the Rancho San Antonio.   Don Larios deeded to the people of San Juan the present cemetery grounds on the road, and with that courtesy that betokens the true Castilian gentleman, divided the tract into two parts, one for a Catholic cemetery, the other a Protestant cemetery.

Those cemeteries now contain the pioneers of the old Mission San Juan Bautista.   A pathetic incident in connection with that cemetery is that when the estimable Don deeded the ground for the cemetery he reserved for his family a piece of ground fronting on the road.   It could be easily distinguished years ago and may be distinguished now, for all I know, by a barbed wire fence that cuts it off from the rest of the cemetery.

This barbed wire fence, it is said, was put around the grave of the donor of the cemetery grounds for an infraction of the rules and regulations governing the cemetery.

Boy-like, when my parents first moved to San Juan, I was timid and afraid of the black-robed padres that governed the mission.   They were a new species of beings to me.   I was very anxious to see the interior of the old mission but I was afraid one of those friars might grab me.   Friars were mysterious objects to me.   One day when I was running around barefooted and passing along the corridor alongside of the church I peeked through one of the windows to see what those strange men were doing.   It must be remembered that, at the time, the padres lived in that long building that fronts the plaza, adjoining the mission church.   Whilst engaged in peeking through the window, to my dismay, a gentle hand touched my shoulder— one of those dreaded padres had stepped silently behind me and I looked up into a face beaming down on mine with kindliness and humor.   He asked me if I was afraid, but one glance at his kindly countenance banished all the fears I had previously felt, and I replied, "No."   The gentle father then invited me to inspect the church; this was something that I had long desired to do but was afraid that if I attempted it misfortune might come to me.   The priest took me through the church explaining the various objects of worship and then took me up into the ancient organ loft where there is to be seen (I suppose it is there yet) an immense bass viol that was made hundreds of years ago by the Indians, also a musical curiosity in the shape of a barrel organ.   This barrel organ was made in London, it was turned by a handle and played, if I remember aright, some three or four tunes.   The first tune that I recollect on this organ was "The Devil's Dance."   When the padres settled at the San Juan Mission the Indians were very timorous and afraid of them.   The legend runs that the organ played an important part in their conversion.   It was brought out and played and the Indians' curiosity overcame their fear in their desire to see what that strange thing was.   Thus the padres got a chance to become acquainted with the Indians and the acquaintanceship ripened into devotion on the part of the aborigines. But, I think, it was a funny thing that the Indians were lured to the shadow of the church by a tune called, "The Devil's Dance." The priest, after showing me these relics of former days, then took me to the enclosure alongside of the church, back of the living quarters of the friars and told me that there were over four thousand bodies buried in that small enclosure which was, to the best of my recollection, about the size of a small town lot. He told me that it took fifteen years to build that old mission church and then he showed me the old building that they used as a place of worship during the building of the mission. This old building, I believe, now stands; it was built at right angles to the present church. The gentle friar invited me to call and see him whenever I came up to the mission. I often visited the good padre. It developed that this friar had a shotgun and was an ardent sportsman. Now, at this time, game of all kinds abounded in the San Juan Valley. On my father's place could be found snipe, and sometimes ducks, and various kinds of feathered game. The priest asked my father for permission to hunt over his land; father gladly consented and told him to come and shoot over his land whenever he liked. One day this priest, starting on one of his shooting trips, had occasion to pass our house. It so happened that just at that time my mother was finishing up a churning and had a large quantity of buttermilk. The priest was very fond of buttermilk and asked my mother if she would give him some. She did and also brought forth a bountiful supply of cake and doughnuts which he greatly enjoyed. This incident brought about a friendship between my parents and this priest which lasted while he was there, and was greatly enjoyed by both parties. He came over to the house nearly every week and my mother was always ready to entertain him with buttermilk or some other luxury which the mission could not afford. This padre's name was Ubach. Years later I had occasion to go to San Diego and, lo, and behold! when I embarked on the steamer at San Francisco, who should I find on the boat but Father Ubach on his way to the old San Diego Mission.   The meeting was a joyful one and we made the trip together.   A gentle, kindly soul!   He has long since passed to his heavenly reward.   I shall always remember him with affection.

Another priest, the late Father Valentin Closa, was almost my spiritual advisor when I would consult him about my friend and neighbor, Mary Ferguson.

Mary Ferguson would start for town with a white rag tied over her head.   We had no radios, but a message would go on the air quicker than radio.   "Mary Ferguson is in town!" and the fellows would disappear.   You couldn't even find the constable with a search warrant.   But I had to eat, occasionally, and Mary would corner me going or coming home and her vocabulary of profane words was something amazing.   It was after one of these encounters that I generally had a talk with Father Closa, who apparently had heard Mary's tongue wag.

So, we were brother members, as it were.   Father Closa was a fine christian gentleman, and many good talks I had with him.   He would advise me not to lose my temper, and I have always been thankful for the counsel that he gave me.

SAN JUAN BAUTISTA ELEMENTARY SCHOOL 1868

CHAPTER III

San Juan's schools, in the early days, were unique—
Teachers were hard to get and hard to keep—
Some of the pioneer teachers.

S I RELATED, at the beginning of these reminiscences, the first school I attended was in Tuolumne
county. The next school that contributed towards
my education was in San Juan. This school district
comprised what is now known as San Benito county, and it
was a school district with an area larger than the whole state
of Rhode Island.

I remember the names of two of the first trustees of that
school district. One was Patrick Breen, the father of the well-
known Breen family who were members of the ill-fated Donner
party. At the time we arrived in San Juan (1855) Mr. Breen
was postmaster and the Breen family resided in the adobe home
once owned by General Castro. This relic of former days,
with its long veranda, still stands alongside the Plaza Hotel.
The other trustee of the school was John Jordan who farmed
a tract of land in the lower end of the valley adjacent to Frank
Ross' place. Jordan was principally engaged in raising hogs.
Frank Ross was afterwards sheriff of San Benito county. I do
not remember the name of the third trustee.

When the school district was first organized they rented
a building; in fact they rented several—first locating the school
here and then there, but finally built the one-story building
that for years was used as a school and which is located at the
lower end of the cemetery property, across on the "Rocks Road."

We had many teachers in that school; men of different
nationalities. The first that I remember was William B. Harris,

a very peculiar man. He was of Cherokee extraction and his father lived in the San Juan Canyon. The next teacher was Mr. Cooper who was followed by the Rev. Azariah Martin, afterwards principal for many years of the Hollister School District. Mr. Martin was a minister (if I remember correctly, of the Methodist denomination).

The first tax levy for school purposes occurred in 1868 to defray the expenses of erecting a school on the site now occupied by the San Juan High School. It must be understood that in those days there were no such things as high schools or grammar schools or universities. All the pupils attended the one teacher who was a male, in fact, generally speaking, all the teachers were men. The people employed whoever they could get to take the job. Sometimes it would be a minister and sometimes a lawyer; men unable to make a living following their professions.

In about four or five months the school money was gone and then school was suspended and sometimes the teacher, if he was able, would start a private school to which my parents would send me. Sometimes the teacher would be Scotch, and at other times Irish. There was, up to the time the school was built, no regular building for holding school. It was usually some private house or church until 1859 when the small school building above alluded to on the "Rocks Road," was built. It is deserted now and has not been used for many years.

In the early sixties, after this schoolhouse was built, there came to San Juan a young man by the name of Samuel Shearer, who applied for the position of teacher. The trustees hired him and he retained the position for a long time. As a teacher Mr. Shearer was second to none. He had the faculty of being able to impart knowledge to pupils so that they would understand it. His hobby was mathematics. There was always a broad smile on his face when he had some of us at the blackboard working at a difficult problem and explaining as we proceeded the whys and wherefores of the operation.

Mr. Shearer taught all the pupils in the school and, as there were too many scholars for one teacher to attend to, properly, the trustees hired an assistant for the smaller pupils. This lady's name was Miss French.

Well do I remember the day she came. Some of the boys including myself, all about the same age, talked it over and we concluded it would be embarrassing for a perfect stranger to take charge of a school like that one. So, we put it up to Mr. Shearer and he advised us to appoint someone to escort her to the school. Simeon Harris was picked to do the honors, as he was about the best dressed pupil. He performed the task with credit to himself.

Simeon Harris was a classmate of mine and a very bright boy. Simeon and Alfred Harris, another schoolmate, were brothers of Dan Harris, the San Juan merchant. Amelia Harris, who also attended the same school was a sister of the above named lads.

The introduction of Mr. Shearer to Miss French rang the bell—not at that particular time, but not so very long after, the wedding bells rang and Miss French became the wife of Samuel Shearer.

On Friday afternoon we had recitations and spelling matches. There were always parents and grownups present to see how we performed. This, I think, had a very good effect on the pupils.

Mr. Shearer afterwards located in Salinas and was elected superintendent of schools in Monterey county. Mr. Shearer was also for a long time a grain broker. [3]

Mr. Shearer died a few years ago. Towards the last of his life he commenced writing a series of reminiscenses which were published in the Salinas Index, and which proved to be highly interesting.

Mr. Shearer was a learned man, and he was mourned, at his passing, by all who knew him. He was one of the early type of educators in this state, and left the impress of his thorough schooling on many of the prominent men that afterwards helped to build up this commonwealth.

Conditions were primitive in those days. The pupils all sat on benches, as the only chair in the room was used by the teacher—a mark of distinction. The pupil or his parents had to make his own desk, consequently the school room possessed a motley aspect as regards desks. My father, who was quite a workman, made my desk. It had the unusual distinction of having a lock on it enabling me to place my lunch in the desk (it is hardly necessary to say that the lunch would have been stolen if it had been left laying around). I also kept my books, safely, in there.

Hygiene was something that no one knew anything about, and as far as hygiene rules were concerned they were fractured— in fact, broken into smithereens. There was no examination of pupils' eyes, throats, or teeth, as we have today. I cite these things in order to show how far we have advanced in everything that makes living worthwhile. And yet, under the simple guidance of these educators, we learned the three R's and learned them well. We all drank out of the same bucket with the same dipper and sometimes the water was anything but pure. In many cases the bucket of water had to be packed a quarter of a mile or so from some pump.

With all my mother's eternal vigilance in the matter, I would, now and then, accumulate a large colony of "cooties," (in those days we called them lice) and then, God help me, I got it good and plenty from my dear mother who, of course, insisted that I had been playing around with some of those "no goods" at school.

The classes in school were made up of all nationalities— Spanish, American, Mexicans and Chilenoes; in fact, almost every nationality on the globe except Chinese and Japanese.

The books were varied, too. We had no series. They were made up of all kinds and of different authors,—Towne's Spelling Book, McGuffey's Readers, Ray's Mental Arithmetic, and J. Davies' Mathematics. Inasmuch as the books that came to California were brought around the Horn (at least a majority of them were) it can be imagined what a strange assortment of books were used in that school. I remember well one old history I had. It was Peter Parley's History and contained biblical stories about David and Goliath, Susan and the Elders, and also stories about George Washington who "never told a lie" and the Battles of Bunker Hill and of Ticonderoga. It contained other stories that were calculated to arouse our patriotism, and to give us a desire for truth and upright living. (I wish to remark right here that in my childish mind there was always a suspicion that the story about George Washington's never telling a lie was the biggest kind of "bunk." Someone told that story so often that he commenced believing it, I always asserted).

Discussing my earlier school days brings back to my memory an incident which reflects early day conditions. In the latter 60's Castroville was a big burg as "burgs" went in those days and, of course, they had a school there. There were large boys attending the school and it may be asserted that the old saying about the "wild west where men are men" might be parodied to the effect that in the early days of California "boys were hellions"—which translated into the vernacular means that they were rough, boisterous, aped the manners of their progenitors and men associates, and ran things generally with a high hand.

This condition of affairs existed in many schools but notably so in the Castroville school. The boys in that school were so rough and turbulent and made it so unpleasant for the teacher that the trustees found it almost impossible to find anyone willing to teach the school. The boys made it so warm and lively for the instructors that the latter usually, after a few weeks' or months' trial at the job, quit in disgust.

At one period in Castroville's history the school trustees engaged a teacher from Monterey. His name was Tom Clay, a nephew of the famous Henry Clay of Congressional fame in the 50's in Washington and one of the principal figures in the lurid discussions in congress that led to our Civil War. Tom Clay said that he would teach the school and in due time it was announced that the school would reopen with a new teacher. The boys prepared to give this new teacher a taste of wild life and intended to hold a jamboree when he was compelled to make his exit from the scene of his labors.

On the morning that the school opened all the pupils attended—boys and girls. The boys were of mature size, many of them could be called young men they were such strapping, muscular young fellows. Tom Clay rang the bell, the pupils trooped in and took their places. Clay proceeded to his desk and after making the pupils recite the Lord's prayer told them to sit down. Then, reaching back to his hip pocket, he pulled out a six-shooter which he regarded fondly and, laying it on the edge of his desk, remarked; "I want all you pupils, especially you young bucks, to understand right now, that I am going to run this school and teach you something. You will do as I say or there is going to be trouble."

History relates that there was no further trouble in that school. The pupils became obedient and "perlite" and Tom Clay retired from his position, as teacher, with added lustre to the name of Clay. *

The San Juan parents sent their children to school to obey the rules and if they were punished for disobedience, they were generally punished again on their return home. My parents considered it a mark of 'disgrace for their children to be whipped for disobeying the rules. They argued that the teacher must have had a good reason for flogging or else he would not have done so and accordingly, Solomon's injunction to "Chastise thy son in his youth so that he may rejoice in his latter end" was followed to the letter by outraged parents.

Of all the pupils that attended the San Juan school when I went to school there, but five remain, one of whom is Fielding Hodges, son of Chas. and Mrs. Hodges who came to San Juan in 1857. Of a family of five children, but three boys remain; Fielding, William and Samuel Hodges. William Hodges has been employed in the assessor's office in Oakland for the past thirty years; Samuel Hodges lives in Hollister on the San Benito river and Fielding Hodges married a daughter of Tile and Mrs. Rupe. They have a fine residence on the west side of Monterey street between Third and Fourth Streets, San Juan. He is a carpenter by trade and is the same booster for San Juan that he was years and years ago.

Mrs. L. E. Mossup, daughter of Dr. Robt. Mathews, was born in Texas in 1848 and came, with her father, to California

---

* (Editor's Note:—Mr. Mylar tells the above story and places the incident at Castroville. He tells us that he got the story from Tom Clay himself. Now, in the early days when we were in Hollister running the Free Lance, we heard the same story but it was located at Fairview. Fairview was known as the Irish District of San Benito County. It contained the families of the Doolings, the Hudner's the Daly's, the Cagneys, and others.

The Fairview school was said to have had the biggest and most turbulent youngsters in all San Benito County. Amongst the pupils were men now prominent and highly respected citizens of San Benito County. The story goes, as told us, that these boys had run every teacher out of that school. It was their pastime. Finally, Tom Clay was engaged to teach and on the morning that he opened the school he laid not one six-shooter, but two six-shooters on the edge of his desk, having extracted the aforesaid artillery from his hip pockets, and remarked, "I understand that you blankety-blank-blanks have been running every teacher out of this school. Well, you can't run me out but, if you think you can, start in just as soon as possible. I am going to run this school and teach you. And if you get rough with me I'm going to kill some of you!" And history says that he taught the school. It became a model school, but those pupils saw to it that he was not re-engaged for another term.

We knew Tom Clay well, in fact, we came near being killed by him one night, but that is another story. Clay was one of Hollister's best-known "characters." His violent antagonism to the churches and their ministers, which he recited on every possible occasion, especially against the Catholic church, made him a village pest who could break up any street gathering quicker than a skunk. Towards his last days Tom took a fancy to the editor of the Pajaronian and we became quite friendly. He was, indeed, a strange character.—Ed. Pajaronian).

in 1852 arriving in November of that year at San Juan. Dr. Mathews traveled overland from Texas to Mazatlan in Mexico where he took passage on a boat to California with his daughter, his wife being deceased. The boat was poorly manned and to make the journey worse a fever broke out amongst the passengers, of which there were four hundred. They soon ran low on water to drink there being only a small tumblerful allowed to each passenger daily. The passengers were dying so rapidly that there were scarcely enough well ones to bury the ones that died. After drifting most of the time, at the end of seventy-two days, they finally landed on Morro Rock, close to San Luis Obispo. Out of the four hundred passengers but five remained besides the sailors.

Dr. Mathews took up his residence in San Juan where Mrs. Mossup grew up and at the age of eighteen married L. A. Mossup in May 1866. Mr. and Mrs. Mossup resided at Bitterwater Valley where they farmed for years. They afterwards moved to Monterey where Mr. Mossup died. Mrs. Mossup is a half sister to the late Sam and John Mathews, who were large stockraisers in Monterey county. Mrs. Mossup owns a comfortable home at 505 Van Buren street, Monterey. Two of her sons, George and Victor live with her. She does her own household work and is cheerful and optimistic.

Another one of my schoolmates is Mrs. Thos. Bickmore of Hollister. Mrs. Bickmore came to San Juan, in 1854 with her stepfather, Dr. Campbell, and her mother. Her mother was a sister of Dr. Robt. Mathews. Mrs. Bickmore's maiden name was Martha Cullumber. Her father died in Arizona and her mother afterwards married Dr. Campbell.

CHAPTER IV.

---

*The pioneer merchandise stores of San Juan—The merchants
who conducted them—Supplies of New Idria Mines were
conveyed by ox teams yoked Spanish style.*

N 1855-1856, San Juan was an important point on
"El Camino Real." Few towns could boast of
more activity than this stopping place for the overland stages. There were four general merchandise
stores; quite a number for so early a period.

One store was conducted by James McMahon, Sr. This
was James McMahon who afterwards built the McMahon
House in Hollister, the leading hostelry in that town, for many
years. It is not necessary to remark that McMahon was an
Irishman. He was the father of Tom McMahon, afterwards
a prominent merchant in Hollister; James who became a law-
yer, and several daughters, one of whom married Judge Jas.
F. Breen, a member of the Breen family of San Juan. Judge
Breen served San Benito county for many years as Superior
Judge.

It was Jas. McMahon, Sr., who purchased the Florence
School at Hollister and presented it to the Catholic Sisters.
This incident is worth relating. I forget what denomination
built that school. It was a fine two-story building on the block
back of the present Catholic church in Hollister. It was intended as a denominational school but did not prosper and
finally the mortgage falling due "Jim" McMahon purchased
the property and presented it to the sisters with the proviso
that it had to be used as a Catholic school, otherwise it would
revert to the McMahon estate. This school is the site of the
present sisters' school at Hollister, and, needless to say, it has
never reverted to the McMahon heirs.

Another store was run by Daniel Harris, a Jew; the third by Mr. Prattalongo, a Frenchman; and the fourth, by Felipe Gardella, an Italian. Accordingly, if you belonged to any one of these four nationalities, you could patronize your own countrymen.

The supplies for these merchandise stores were brought by wagons from Alviso, at the head of San Francisco Bay, to which point they were conveyed by a small flat bottomed steamboat from San Francisco. There was a great deal of freight in those days, as there was a large district to be supplied with goods. Mr. Harris had a contract to furnish the supplies for the New Idria Quicksilver Mining Company, located sixty-nine miles south of Hollister, at that time just across the Fresno County line.

Right here let me interpolate that Fresno county played a low-down trick when it allowed the legislature to cede the New Idria mining district over to San Benito county. At the time of the ceding and for years previous, the New Idria mines were worked by Mexicans and other classes of labor that were prone to killings, fighting, brawls, and general turbulence. There was great interest taken in Hollister in the matter when the cession of this territory was proposed, and all hands except Tom Hawkins, of the Hollister bank, were in favor of it. Fresno county put up a bluff that it would fight losing any of its territory, but after the deal was made it was learned that secretly Fresno politicians and business men favored getting rid of the district. After San Benito took over New Idria it was found that the attitude of the Fresnoans was founded on the fact that killings and brawls up at the mines had cost the county thousands of dollars. I do not know what murders and brawls have cost San Benito county since she has taken over the territory, but she has paid dearly for accepting the trust. I remember one trial of two Mexican boys who murdered a roadside innkeeper near the mines that cost San Benito county upwards of $10,000, and this trial was only a sample of many others that have occurred in the past thirty-five years.

It will be remembered that the New Idria Mines gave Tom Bell, the San Francisco capitalist, (whose tragic history was mixed up with Mammy Pleasant, his negress housekeeper) his start for the great fortune that at one time he held. Harris, the San Juan merchant, would send the goods up to New Idria by pack train and the horses and mules would return with flasks of quicksilver. Anyone acquainted with quicksilver realizes the strength necessary to pick up one of the flasks of that heavy metallic fluid. Some of the animals were compelled to carry three flasks which amounted to about 350 pounds. [4]

These flasks, when brought to San Juan, were carelessly thrown into the yard back of Mr. Harris' store. Although a high-priced commodity, being largely used in mining operations, no one ever stole any of the flasks. Their dead weight precluded anyone from getting any distance with a flask to say nothing of the difficulty in trying to sell the stolen property.

Harris enjoyed this patronage from the mines until it was taken to Gilroy but subsequently a semblance of a road having been constructed to the mines, a Spaniard (whose name I can't remember now) got the contract to do the hauling from Mr. Harris. This Spaniard used oxen, worked Spanish style, that is, the yoke almost straight up, fastened behind and to the horns by a rawhide strap one and one-half inches wide and about eight feet long. The load was pulled altogether by the heads of the poor animals. It took two men to drive a team.

One day out of curiosity I asked one of the drivers why they did not work them American style (with the yoke and bow) to which the driver, in true Spanish style explained that using his method the oxen seemed stronger inasmuch as they "had the strength of the head and the neck to pull the load."

As I said before it took two men to drive a team of oxen and then they could not keep the beasts in the road. Where the road passed our place there was a corner. It was wide and commodious yet notwithstanding this facility, scarcely a trip did this team make that a portion of our fence would not be torn down by the team in making the turn. My brother, who was about 17 years old, decided to lighten his labor of having to repair the fence so often by stopping this damage. Accordingly he cut down an oak tree which had two limbs sticking out. The tree was about two feet through. This he planted at the corner about four feet in the ground. After that no further damage was done to our fence but, oh, Lord, the language that was used by those drivers. I understood Spanish and used to take great delight in hearing their strong language.

After the road was fixed up and opened to some extent, Americans began to use six-horse teams and freighting became general.

SANDSTONE BUILDINGS, CONSTRUCTED CIRCA 1868
Photo circa 1894

CHAPTER V

The San Justo Rancho and how it came to be purchased by
Flint, Bixby and Hollister—The San Juan Lane—
The Killing of Spitts and Bixby

THINK it was in 1854 or 1855, I am not clear about the date, that Dr. Thos. Flint, Llewllyn Bixby, Ben Flint and W. W. Hollister bought what was known as the San Justo Rancho. This rancho comprised over one-half of the San Juan Valley and extended from below our place over to the Santa Ana Valley. Its width comprised from the Bolsa (through which the S. P. R. R. line now runs) across the top of what was afterwards known as the "Flint Hills" to the low hill at the base of the Gabilan range and contained 35,619 acres. Between this row of hills and the Gabilan range is located what is known as the San Juan Canyon. [5]

Hollister, at that time, lived on the site of what afterwards was Dr. Flint's home. Dr. Flint lived close to Hollister on the site of what was afterwards known as Straube's place but which site has long since been washed away by freshet flows of the river. The San Justo Rancho, as it was then known, and which was a great domain, was owned by the Pacheco family after whom the Pacheco Pass is now named. Don Pacheco got this ranch as a grant from the Mexican government. At the time that Flint, Bixby et al., bought the rancho there were quite a number of squatters on the land but, most of these squatters, finding it useless to endeavor to set up any title to their holdings, moved away peaceably. Still, however, there were some of the squatters who held hard feelings against the new owners of the land and nourished a grudge against them. This nourished grudge resulted in a mysterious killing which has never been satisfactorily explained. One of the men credited with being greatly incensed at having to remove, was a man by the name of Florence Spitts.

At this point it would be well to comment on the creation of the road between San Juan and Hollister, known ever since its creation as "The San Juan Lane." After purchasing the San Justo Rancho, which was not fenced, in any way, owing to the fact that people were making roads and lanes here and there and everywhere, it became necessary to create a main thoroughfare through this new holding. It was aimed to connect with the New Idria road which is now but a trace of what it was in those days. The New Idria road was on the west side of the San Benito river. Owing to some miscalculation the lane was not placed on the township line, as first intended. However it was surveyed and then it became necessary to fence it. This necessity was brought about by the fact that droves of cattle were roaming everywhere and the rancho was bought primarily by the Flint, Bixby Co., and Hollister for the purpose of giving their respective flocks of sheep the rich succulent grasses that grew throughout that region. It will be remembered that Dr. Flint brought from the East, across the plains, a large body of sheep as narrated in his diary, published in the Pajaronian, some time ago. Mr. Hollister also brought a large band of sheep across the plains from the east. When the fencing was undertaken Hollister built his fence on the south side of the road placing the posts on the outside next to the road, and palings were nailed onto these posts. It was a rough looking fence. The north side of the road was fenced in a very workmanlike manner by Flint & Bixby. They put up neat looking posts and topped them with palings. Such was the condition of affairs when a dissolution of co-partnership occurred, and the San Justo Rancho holdings were divided.[6] In order to understand this matter it would be well to state that the division of the rancho ran very nearly north and south. The boundary line between the two holdings was placed at or near the vicinity of what is now known as the "Bonnie Brae Orchard." Mr. Hollister took the southern portion of the rancho

and Flint & Bixby the northern portion.   There was a difference in Hollister's favor in the division of the rancho worth
$10,000 which money was paid over to him by Flint & Bixby.

Some time after the San Justo Rancho was divided between
Flint, Bixby & Co., and Hollister, a terrible tragedy occurred
on the San Juan Lane at what was commonly known as the
"Middle of the Lane."

At that point there stood a house that had been built
by one of the squatters, and around it had been also erected
a number of sheep corrals, or sheds.   The Flint, Bixby Co.,
kept a flock of sheep there.   A young brother of Llewllyn Bixby
had come from the east and Llewllyn placed him at this house
in charge of the sheep—I have forgotten this younger brother's
name.   He was about 19 years of age.[7]

Florence Spitts, who was one of the original settlers on
the San Justo Rancho, after its purchase by the Flint, Bixby
Co., and Hollister, settled east of the present city of Hollister
somewhere out in the Santa Ana Valley section where he
found some government land and took it up.   He always came
to San Juan for his supplies.

One day making a visit to San Juan, on leaving that town,
he arrived about sun-down at my father's place.   I remember
this incident well because my father, my brother and I were
milking cows in the barn yard, when he rode in on our place.
I noticed in particular that he had a churn-dasher tied to the
back of his saddle.   He had seemed ill-humored and ready for
a warm argument.   He stayed at our place but a short time and
started homeward.

The next morning a passerby coming along the lane found
the front gate belonging to the house occupied by young Bixby
torn from its fastenings and lying in the middle of the road,
presumably wrenched from its fastenings by a lariat attached
to the pommel of a saddle.   In the middle of a corral, in front
of the house was found Spitts' horse shot dead.   At the rear

of the house by the side of a door there was a barrel.   Sitting, leaning against this barrel, was the body of Spitts who had been shot through the stomach.   Spitts had not been dead long as his body was still warm; his pistol was lying alongside of him.

Spitts had taken his belt off after being shot and loosening his clothes tried to stop the flow of blood which covered a large portion of the porch.   In taking his belt off, he had dropped his pistol which had been discharged—all six chambers being empty.   Inside the door of the room, which was the kitchen, with his feet toward the door lay the body of young Bixby who had been shot through the neck underneath the jaw, killing him instantly.

There were bullet holes through the front door of the house and also through the rear door.   The killings to this day have remained a mystery, but investigators who looked into the matter evolved the theory that Spitts, riding home, in ill-humor, engaged in some sort of an altercation with young Bixby.   The altercation extended to the rear of the house where Spitts was shot, and that when Bixby opened the door to see where his antagonist was, Spitts, ready for him, killed him instantly.

Although killings in those days were common occurrences this mysterious affair caused great excitement.

The sale of the San Justo Rancho was consummated about 1855, but, in order to keep the records straight, let me state here that some of these settlers, on the rancho, or as they were known in those days, "squatters;" did not commence to move off the rancho until about 1857-'58.   Many of these settlers moved away from the valley and were never heard from again.   I cannot recall the names of all these settlers, but as near as I remember now, the first settler's house was on the south side of the valley, going towards Hollister, and was originally built by a family by the name of Francis (Bob Francis' father and mother).   It was at this place that, subsequently, I got the lambs narrated elsewhere.

The father of Bob Francis was a shoemaker, and after he died my father bought his shoe-making tools. Mrs. Francis died in the valley and Bob returned to the east and was never heard from again.

A little farther along in the valley I should judge about a half mile, or so, Andrew Abbe lived.

The next place was occupied by a man by the name of Brandon. Brandon afterwards took charge of the toll-house on the Pacheco Pass road. He maintained a roadside inn there.

After Brandon's death his widow married Cy Dubois, a horseman and trader who followed the races. Mr. Dubois was well known throughout the San Juan and Santa Clara Valleys. After their marriage, Mr. and Mrs. Dubois resided for a while in San Jose.

The next place was Florence Spitts', whose tragic death we have mentioned previously. He lived at the mouth of a canyon, which was always known, and is still known, as "Spitts' Canyon."

The next settler to Spitts was a man by the name of Pennypacker. He lived on the land that George Moore subsequently acquired from the Hollister subdivision.

Through the middle of the valley, about where the lane runs now, was located the home of Benjamin Wilcox. Wilcox's home was located on the north side of the valley.

About a stone's throw from the lane, where it is now located, was a place occupied by William Thorne. Mr. Thorne's wife died there in 1857.

There were a few other settlers on the San Justo Rancho at the time but they moved away and I have forgotten their names. [8]

On the north side of the valley, near the bank of the San Benito river, lived a family by the name of Crooks. Their place was situated about a half mile above where Ben Flint afterwards lived.   Mr. Crooks had married a sister of the well-known Watson brothers, Dave, Steve, Henry and the rest of them.   Crooks had a son about my age, a schoolmate, who was named Cassius.   He was named after Cassius M. Clay, the distinguished member of Congress.   After leaving the San Justo Rancho, Crooks and his family moved to Grass Valley, otherwise known as the Cienega.   This is the valley that gives Hollister its present water supply.

On the opposite side of the San Benito River from Crooks' place, there lived a family by the name of Campbell.   Mr. Campbell married a widow by the name of Cullumber, who was a sister of Dr. Mathews and "Uncle Johnny" of San Benito. "Uncle Johnny" Mathews was the Democratic assemblyman, for many terms, for San Benito county after it was created, and was one of the finest, squarest, and most honorable men that ever sat in the assembly chamber at Sacramento. [9]   John, Sam, and Martha Cullumber were schoolmates of mine at San Juan.   Martha Cullumber afterwards married a man by the name of Bickmore.   The Bickmore family lived at Corralitos, in Santa Cruz county.   In passing let me remark that Martha was a splendid girl.

At the Campbell place commenced a road that ran directly over into the San Joaquin Valley.   It was used by the people of San Juan for several years.   This road skirted the low hills to a point and then struck directly to the Pacheco adobe, on the south bank of Pacheco creek, and thence through the Pass into the San Joaquin Valley.   This was a main traveled thoroughfare in those days.

Benjamin Wilcox, after moving off the San Justo Rancho, purchased a plot of ten acres on the west side of the Alameda. He erected a nice house on it.   The plans for this house were drawn by George Chalmers, brother of Alec Chalmers who built the Pajaro Valley National Bank building, and many other notable structures in the early days of Watsonville. Chalmers, in the construction of the house, was assisted by

Wilcox' sons Edward and Sylvester Wilcox, who were carpenters. Joseph Wilcox plastered the edifice and did the inside work. The house had a cutstone foundation. As I passed this building every day going to and coming from school, I watched the progress of its construction. Little did I think, at that time, that it would play such an important part in my life. It was here, soon after the Wilcox family moved into their new home, that I saw a little girl playing around in the yard. This little girl afterwards became my wife.

Benjamin Wilcox word was as good as his bond. There never lived a more square or more honorable gentleman. He was born in New York in 1796, and died in New York City in 1870. He died from heart prostration on a visit to New York which he made with his wife, who was afflicted with a cancer on the eye and for whom he sought treatment from a specialist. Mrs. Wilcox returned and did not die until two years later.

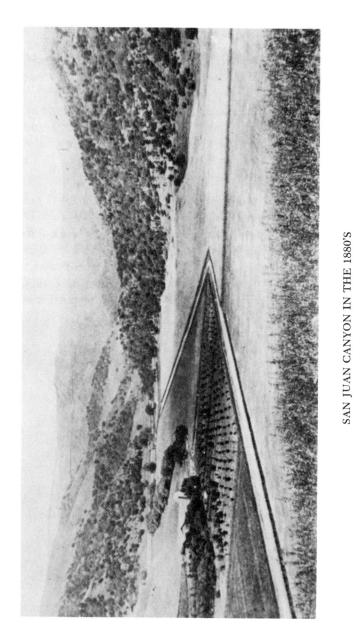

SAN JUAN CANYON IN THE 1880'S

CHAPTER VI

The roads to and from San Juan were very rough in the early days—Many bad characters—Summary justice meted out to criminals by Judge Lynch

AN JUAN was visited in the middle of the '50's by every wayfarer travelling north or south. We were on "El Camino Real" for sure. There was no other road up or down the coast except by the Tejon Pass, beyond Bakersfield, and very few traveled that route. At that time there were no houses in the San Joaquin Valley, no accommodations were to be had and it was naturally a very hard and toilsome route. The missions seemed to have been established a certain distance apart and as there was always someone living around them it made it more comfortable and convenient for travelers. From San Juan to Santa Clara Mission was about 45 miles; from San Juan to Monterey about 40 miles; from San Juan to Soledad Mission, also about 40 miles, and so on, down the coast, making them within a day's journey of each other.

The peculiar fact about that road was that it was all a perfectly natural road—that is, it was easy to travel notwithstanding the fact that from one end to the other, it was never looked after by any road crew.

All the things I missed when out of school I saw while in school because the road passed the school house and we missed nothing. There would be the "carretta" or wooden cart, with wheels of solid wood six inches thick and about five feet high with a hole in the center through which a big wooden axle, with a tongue, was inserted. A bed was put on this and some standards set up to carry the rawhide top which was very heavy and rough. Under this top, on rude seats, sat the women and children. The vehicle was drawn by two yoke of oxen as one yoke of oxen would have had a hard time pulling the cart alone. Often you could hear these "carrettas" squeaking long before, and after, you could see them, crying for lack of grease. The men generally rode on horseback. Then there would be covered wagons going south drawn by horses in which rode Americans looking for homes. It was no wonder that all of California's bandits could be traced to San Juan during some part of their career. Murietta, "Three-Fingered Jack," Vasquez, and Chavez, were frequent visitors to the town.

Chavez, as a boy lived at San Juan. I knew him well and played marbles with him many times. He was a hard-looking boy, almost like an Indian, not a bad boy but rough, thick-necked, dark and heavy set.

Although Vasquez went to school at San Juan, I did not know him then. I saw him time and again in after years. The bandits would stay, during the day, in the upper story of the buildings along Fourth street, which was known as the "waterfront" and come out and prowl around the streets at night. We never said anything to them for fear of reprisals.

There were others in the town that could be called bad men, but the American population that had settled in and around the town had a way of handling them that made them good citizens. I found that out one morning on my way to school.

I had to travel along what was called "The Alameda"—a street or road that extended out in our direction and had been planted with willows on each side, by the padres, a certain distance apart. They had grown to be large trees during all those years. At some time in the long distant past, "The Alameda" had been paved with brick by the padres for I had noticed here and there remnants of the bricks protruding through the dust. One of these trees in particular had a limb extending over the road and on this morning as I was skipping along to school I was horrified to see the body of a man suspended from this limb.

It developed that this was the body of a man who, the night previous, had killed one of the Flint-Bixby sheep-herders. The sheep-herder came into town that night and displayed some twenty-five dollars or so.   This excited the cupidity of the man whose body I saw.   He stealthily followed the sheep-herder as the latter proceeded homeward, and killed him with a picket which he wrenched from the nearby fence.   It so happened that he killed the sheep-herder underneath this same tree.   The crime was traced to the man by a band of the citizens, "Vigilantes," as they were styled in those days, who administered summary justice by hanging him to the tree.

Another time I saw two bodies hanging from this same tree.   I am proud to say, looking back, that in all my life I never took part in any mob, or in any scene of violence although nearly every mob act that I witnessed at San Juan was to my thinking justified, and you may well believe that San Juan in the early days was the scene of much lawlessness and crime.

Another time, proceeding to school, in the morning, I saw, near this same tree on "The Alameda," a man's hat.   I commenced looking around and peering over a fence into a ditch, I saw the body of a murdered man in the running water. He had been shot through the right temple and was instantly killed.   The pistol had been placed almost against the skin, for his temple was powder-marked, and both murderer and victim must have been mounted at the time the deed was done.

Badly scared I ran into town and reported my find.   Citizens went out, recovered the body, and held an inquest, but so far as I know the mystery was never solved—who the murdered man was and who killed him.   Connor Hickey, who lived up in the San Juan Canyon, going home late the night before had seen two Mexicans.   These Mexicans were arrested but as nothing could be proved against them they were released.

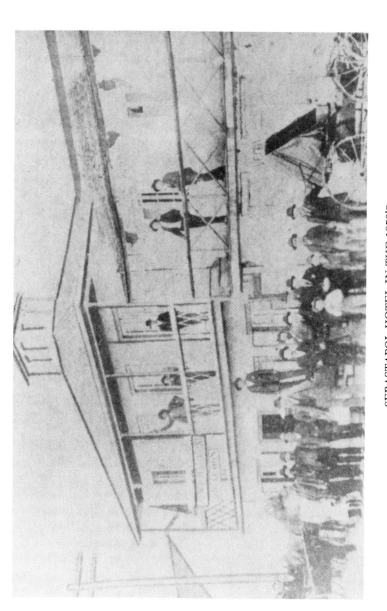

SEBASTAPOL HOTEL IN THE 1850'S

CHAPTER VII

*The Streets in San Juan in its Early Days, and those who
lived on the principal thoroughfares—Some of
the Pioneer Merchants*

T THIS point I desire to take up the layout of the
streets of San Juan Bautista as they were in my
boyhood days.

First Street is the street on which the present
high school is located; Second Street is the street which leads
up to the plaza; Third Street was and still is the principal
street of San Juan; Fourth Street was commonly known as
the "Waterfront."

In other words the traveler coming from San Jose came
along First Street to the outskirts of the town where he de-
bouched in on Second Street which led up to the plaza; or, if
he did not intend going to the Plaza Hotel, or the old Mission,
he turned still farther west and struck the main thoroughfare,
Third Street.

Now on this main thoroughfare were located in the early
days (1856) the following stores and residences:

Going from my home to school the first big place on the
left was a large adobe structure occupied by the Castro family.
The place was noted for the beautiful flowers that grew in the
front yard. I remember that I often asked the women of that
household for some of the flowers which they generously bestowed upon me. On the opposite side of the street from the
Castro residence was a small house occupied by a French woman
named Madame Azul. Adjoining the Madame's holdings was
the residence of Samuel Breen, brother of Patrick Breen, Sr.

On the left again, on the corner of Franklin and Third
Streets was a square adobe used as a dwelling at that time and
since then for many other purposes. Next to this adobe came

a vacant lot, then another adobe in the shape of an "L" which extended along Third Street to a certain point, and then down Washington Street.   It was a saloon at that date, and although used for many other purposes since my boyhood days, it is still standing.

The saloon was conducted by one John Forney.   I remember one incident that occurred when Forney got married.   A marriage in those days was a notable event and consequently the boys determined to give Forney a good sendoff.

There was an old cannon lying on the ground in the plaza that was used for Fourth of July celebrations and other festive occasions.   The boys took this old muzzle-loader down about midnight and placed it on the porch of Forney's saloon.   At a given signal they touched the cannon off and it blew every pane of glass in the house to smithereens!

A seven-days wonder in San Juan, just then, was—what did the boys load that cannon with?

Forney was game.   He invited the boys in and treated them to champagne and then some more.   The celebration was long-remembered for many of the participants in that "blow-out," did not sober up from it for two weeks after.

It was in this saloon that Gregorio Sanchez killed John Hopper in self-defense.   The quarrel between the two men culminated in Hopper's attacking Sanchez with a pick-handle and Gregorio "acted quick."

Years after the saloon was the scene of a very funny incident.   I have mentioned elsewhere, in this narrative Ex-Sheriff Frank Ross.   The incident I am about to relate occurred a long time after Forney's wedding, when the saloon was run by Mr. Filoucheau, who was the agent for the vineyard products of Theophile Vache.   It will be remembered by some of the readers of these memoirs, that for years, possibly twenty years if not longer, one of the noted landmarks in San Benito county was the Palmtag vineyard, located on the Bird Creek road, nine miles from San Juan.   This vineyard was originally set out in the early days, when Monterey county covered that entire section now known as San Benito county.   Vache was a Frenchman who had learned vine growing and wine making in his native land, and he set out a beautiful vineyard, from which he manufactured claret, port, white wine and the best brand of brandy that ever crossed one's lips.   Filoucheau, who conducted a saloon in San Juan, was his agent and Vache would send down from his vineyard, in a carretta, two or three barrels of his products, and leaving them with Filoucheau for disposal, the Mexican driver would return on that toilsome journey, there being hardly a vestige of a road through the canyon, to the vineyard, late at night, and, without a mishap.   I have often seen him doing this, and marvelled much at his dexterity, or good luck, which ever it was.   Vache ultimately sold this vineyard to a Hollister banker, the late Wm. Palmtag, who, in turn, after bringing the vineyard up to a high state of development sold it to an eastern capitalist, John H. Dickinson.   Dickinson improved the place greatly, and finally sold it to other parties.

In Filoucheau's saloon there was an instrument of torture used at that time for scraping the tacks out of the soles of boots. It was called the "float," and was a sort of rasp, that, when the tacks protruded through the soles of the boots, enabled one to insert into the boot and rasp the points of the protruding tacks off.

This "float" was kept on the counter.   Frank Ross who was farming in the lower end of the valley, at the time, strayed into the saloon, one day, and met some five or six other congenial spirits.   Hospitality was on tap and liquor flowed freely. Finally, out of a heated argument between Frank and the bunch, a concerted attack was made on Ross by the gang.   Frank, who was about as fearless a man as ever stood in shoe leather, disdaining to pull his gun which he always carried, reached for the "float" and with it laid out two of his attackers.   Whereupon the remainder of the bunch fled.   Frank looked around the room and then addressed his fallen foes with, "Damn you! Why don't the rest of you come on?"

This incident was the laugh of San Juan for a long time.

In proceeding along Third Street, on the right-hand side, we first came to a blacksmith and wheelwright shop on the corner of Franklin and Third Streets, conducted by Jasper Twitchell. That building was an anomaly in San Juan as it was a wooden house standing amidst so many adobe edifices.

The next building in the same block, on the corner of Washington and Third Streets, was a gunsmith store conducted by a Frenchman named Durin. It was a two-story building and Durin was always profitably employed, as he was the only man in town who had a lathe, at that time, and turned out a great deal of lathe work. Durin's place was a rallying point for all the Frenchmen wherein they gathered to celebrate the Fall of the Bastile. I admit that, after I had gained my majority, I used to take delight in attending these affairs. Frenchmen, when celebrating, are proverbially hospitable and I used to enjoy their singing and good fellowship.

On the southeast corner of Washington and Third Streets, proceeding towards the north, was a vacant lot. This vacant lot was backed by the Castro residence (occupied by the Breen family), on Second Street.

Then came a livery stable. My earliest recollection of this livery stable was that it was conducted by a Jew named Wise. This livery stable eventually became the property of Comfort & Zanetta, who annexed it to, and made it a part of, the Plaza Hotel, when the hotel was conducted by that firm.

Proceeding back to the west side of Third Street: Across Washington Street—that is, on the corner of Washington and Third Streets, was an old two-story adobe building owned by Adolphe Vache, brother of Theophile Vache. It was occupied at different times by various merchants. At one time Vache conducted a bakery in it. So many different people occupied it that I cannot recall their names. Upstairs was a small hall that they used for dances, and shows. In fact, this upper story was the first theatre that San Juan had. It was called "Tuccoletta Hall," and was the scene of many "wild" parties.

Next to this building was an adobe in which was conducted a horseshoeing business. This was run by Edward Breen, a son of Samuel Breen. Samuel Breen was a brother to Patrick Breen. Edward Breen was a happy-go-lucky chap who was forever playing tricks on luckless wights.

The building next to Breen's shop was a long, narrow, adobe structure, occupied by a Frenchman, who conducted therein a jewelry store. This man's name, if I remember aright, was Chatlaine. To gain admittance to this building you had to descend two steps. I remember the place very well for, in my school days, whether going or coming, I always stopped in front of that shop and looked at an old-time chronometer in the display window. This chronometer had a pendulum about six inches in diameter and it moved so slowly that, actually, I would watch it for quite a length of time expecting it to stop—but it never stopped. It ran right along until the old Frenchman died. The late Dr. Cargill got that clock, and blamed if it ever ran again, although it was a fine piece of workmanship and up to the time the old man died had maintained splendid time.

Next to this old Frenchman's place was the Sebastopol Hotel; a square building two stories high, conducted by Angelo Zanetta, who had moved to San Juan from Monterey.

In the bar-room of this hotel there was a six-pocket billiard table that had been brought around the horn in a sailing vessel, in 1855.

In this hotel was born, Ernest Zanetta, known throughout the west as "CC" Zanetta; now, and for years past, the constable of San Juan township. Ernest Zanetta married Clara Abbe, daughter of Andrew Abbe, the well-known pioneer of San Juan and one of the original settlers on the San Justo Rancho.

Around the billiard table, in the above mentioned hotel, transpired much more than billiard matches. It was around this table that Andrew Barker fought Frank DeBard. DeBard came out of the fracus with a cut that extended from the tip of his ear to the point of his chin, an inch lower and his throat would have been cut. It made a hideous, nasty-looking scar, that he carried through life. Afterwards, in the bar-room of this building, Joseph Wilcox was shot and killed by Greg Sanchez who fired at Wilcox through the door. Sanchez, after expending a large sum of money, was released, owing to the fact that the quarrel began in a drunken brawl and it was fifty-fifty as to who was the aggressor; also that Wilcox, who lived several days after being wounded, expressed an earnest desire that in case of his death Sanchez would not be prosecuted.

Next to the Sebastopol Hotel, located on the corner of Mariposa and Third Streets, was another adobe building occupied by Pratolongo, a Frenchman. He conducted therein a general merchandise store. This store was afterwards conducted by another Frenchman named Dolleguy.

All the stores kept a barrel of liquor on tap in the rear of the premises for the accommodation of their patrons. The liquor was sold by the gallon and quart, but alongside the barrel there was always to be found a glass. Their patrons, whether invited or not, to do so, could go to the rear of the premises and get a drink.

Across Mariposa Street, from Pratolongo's store on the northeast corner of Third and Mariposa Streets, was the store of Daniel Harris. It was a large building principally adobe. Mr. Harris dealt in general merchandise and had a large trade. Adjoining Harris' store on the west side of Third Street was a long two-story building, and, if I remember aright, it had two steps leading down to the first floor which contained a saloon with a billiard table, also there was a restaurant in the rear of the first floor. The upper story contained a hall that was used for dancing. I remember this hall distinctly as it was there that I took my first lesson in dancing, at a cascaroni ball.

I forget the name of the first man that ran this place, but later on it was conducted by Luis Raggio, Sr. It was in the saloon in this building that one night Bart Taylor was shot in the shoulder by Pablo German. That day there had been a horse race at San Juan, the principal contenders being Cal Ross and the German brothers, Pablo, Chino and Felipe.

Cal Ross was the brother of Annie Ross who afterwards became the wife of the late Hy Woods of Watsonville. There was bad blood between Cal Ross and the German brothers over the outcome of the race as Ross' horse had beat Germans' racer. The shooting was extremely dramatic and highly sensational. I can vouch for this as I was in the saloon at the time the shots were fired.

All hands were crowded around the billiard table on which a rondo game was being conducted. Everyone in the place except myself, a mere stripling, was in a hilarious mood as a great deal of liquor had been consumed over the outcome of the horse race. Cal Ross, anticipating trouble with the Germans yet not wishing to bring on an encounter, had laid his pistol belt aside and tying his six-shooter to a string on his left side under his coat, was acting as gamekeeper. Suddenly one of the German boys clasped Cal around the waist pinning his hands to his sides and a shot was fired, at him, but missing him struck Taylor.

The Germans evidently thought that Cal was unarmed but when the man holding Cal felt the pistol he gave the alarm and they fled. As soon as Cal got loose he drew his revolver and commenced firing. The Germans returned the fire and although the place was decidedly crowded everyone miraculously escaped except old man Raggio who was burned along the neck by one of the bullets, leaving a red mark. Raggio, thinking himself shot, dropped to the floor, behind the counter, and came up, instantly, with two six-shooters, one in each hand, with which he contributed to the gaiety of the occasion.

There was an old Chinese gong in the room with which they were accustomed to summon guests to meals and one of the bullets striking this gong, considerable confusion ensued.

It was certainly a night to be remembered!

In passing let me state that old man Raggio, afterwards ran the principal butcher shop in San Juan, and also one in Hollister, some time later. He was one of San Benito county's supervisors for a period, and an honorable and courteous gentleman. He was one of California's oldest pioneers, coming to this state from Mexico when but a boy, and he worked long and laboriously in Mexico before coming to San Juan.

I forget the year in which the following incident occurred but I remember that at one time a Mexican, who had come to Raggio's saloon drunk, ran amuck.

The Mexican, crazy drunk, wanted to shoot somebody and with a pistol in hand emerged from the saloon announcing his determination. Everyone in sight disappeared. He proceeded along the street to the corner of Third Street. There, coming around the corner he met a Mexican, Manuel Butron, who used to have epileptic fits. The drunk-crazed Mexican fired point-blank at Manuel, shooting him squarely through the center of the breast. A crowd of citizens gathered and took the shooter into custody. Manuel laid on the ground, and with every breath he took the blood spurted in the air, coupled with the escaping air from his lungs.

'Twas a pitiful sight! Everyone present said, "Adios, Manuel!" and in their minds as there being no hope of Manuel's recovering, they concluded to finish up the business speedily, Accordingly, they announced that they would take the Mexican down to the willow tree on "The Alameda" and hang him.

In accordance with the request of the Mexican who, to a certain extent, had come to his senses, and wanted a priest, the mob sent up to the mission and brought a priest down. After the priest had interviewed the man, the crowd took him down to "The Alameda" and hanged him.

But here is a strange quip of fortune—Manuel Butron not only recovered from the wound but never had any fits after that. The man who was hanged should really have received compensation for his surgical operation instead of having to "shuffle off his mortal coil." The hanging of that man, after Manuel got well, rested heavily on the consciences of some of the men that so promptly executed summary justice on the poor devil.

KEMP HOME BUILT IN THE 1860'S

CHAPTER VIII

The various dwellings on San Juan streets in 1855-1870, *and
who occupied them—John Bigley, one of the mission's
early teamsters and a man highly respected*

HE PLACE next to Raggio's dwelling was a small
adobe occupied by Mrs. Jesus Bernal, who kept
therein a little restaurant and accommodated a few
lodgers. The rest of the property along the street
for a quarter of a block contained a number of small buildings
which were owned by Felipe Gardella.

I remember Felipe Gardella well. He was the first man
I saw in San Juan on that memorable trip that my parents
took from Calaveras County as far as the Salinas River. Reaching San Juan we halted for a short time and I, peering out
of the covered wagon, saw Gardella seated by the roadside with
a little drum of coffee which he was parching over a small fire.
The coffee inside of his drum was slowly revolved by a handle
which Gardella turned. He had a little store where he sold
knicknacks, notions, tobaccos, etc. Hanging inside of the door
of his store was a green parrot, a bird that greatly attracted
my curiosity. I also remember that green parrot well in after
years, for he and I became the best of friends, and when he saw
me passing the store, either going or coming, he would whistle
and call, "Here, Ikey! Here, Ikey!"

In the early '70's, all along that west side of Third Street
was burned down in a disastrous fire. The fire stopped this
side of the building now occupied by Lavagnino's store.

The brick building the Abbe Company now occupy was
built by Gardella before the fire and occupied by Dan Harris,
after the fire, until he moved from San Juan. The building
that we have previously referred to in this narrative as having

been occupied by Mr. Filoucheau was subsequently taken over by the Bowie brothers who bought Filoucheau's stock and opened up a business there.   Afterwards they moved to the brick building erected by Gardella and took over Sam Harris' stock contained therein.

After Gardella's death, Mrs. Gardella sold the brick building to the Abbe family, the Bowies built a building across the street, moved their stock over there and conducted a general merchandise business therein until they died.

Retracing our steps across the east side of Third Street, we find at the corner of Mariposa Street and Third Street, a building occupied by Leon Bullier, a barber.   I will say right here that in speaking of many of these buildings such as Bullier's, they were not adobe buildings.   They were a sort of stucco affair, i. e., uprights were run up, say two stories high, and mud blocks were inserted between them.   Then there was an outside and inside coating for all this mud and the same was whitewashed and when nicely fixed up was very inviting, having all the characteristics and appearance of an adobe building.

Bullier's place was afterwards occupied by Breitbarth's Shoe Store.

Next to the Bullier building was a saloon, run at different times, by various Mexicans.   At one time one of the members of the Roza family ran it.   Next door there was a bakery, conducted by a Frenchman; then a small building which was occupied by old man Bowie.

The Bowie family were Scotch-Canadians, coming from Canada.   This building occupied by old man Bowie was built for him by my father and John Miller, of Monterey.   The prevailing wage in those days was $2.00 and $2.50 per day, of ten hours.   It was a frame structure and the business that Mr. Bowie engaged in was a bakery.   At the time that old man Bowie was conducting this store, the rest of his family, his sons and daughters, had not yet arrived at San Juan.   Quite a while after the old couple settled there, the sons and daughters joined their parents.

Joe Bowie, one of the sons, was an expert accountant and for a time worked at his calling at San Jose and in the New Almaden quicksilver mines where he was also a Deputy Sheriff of Santa Clara County.

There were four daughters in the Bowie family. The eldest of the quartette was a very finely educated woman who not only taught French and music but also taught school at San Juan for a long time. I went to school to her, and we used to call her, "Aunt Eliza." Another daughter married "Jim" Sargent; the third married Wesley Smith and the other daughter married a man by the name of Hall. One of the Wesley Smith's daughters married Dr. Thos. Flint's son, Richard.

Adjoining the Bowie Bakery there was a vacant lot, after which came a building conducted as a bowling alley by James Miller. Next to this bowling alley was a building in which a butcher shop was conducted by Bill Byrd.

Bill Byrd afterwards moved to the Pajaro Valley and conducted a saloon on the "Lovering Corner" long before Second Street was put through from Rodriguez Street to Main Street. At the time that Bill conducted that saloon in Watsonville there was only a small alley that allowed ingress and egress between Main and Rodriguez Streets. Bill Byrd had a brother named James Byrd who also lived in the Pajaro Valley.

These were all the buildings at that time (1856) on that block, to the corner of Polk Street in San Juan.

In the next block on the corner of Third and Polk Streets there was a building occupied by James McMahon's General Merchandise Store. McMahon's building was erected after we settled in San Juan. Previous to its erection, McMahon had been conducting a business in partnership with a man by the name of Griffin, if I remember correctly, somewhere on Second Street.

After the partnership was dissolved, McMahon engaged my father and Miller to build not only the above store for him but a residence for his family on Second and Polk Streets. These buildings were erected in 1857.

On the corner of Third Street and Mokelumne Street, there was a residence occupied by the Bowie family.

Across Mokelumne Street, from Mokelumne Street to San Jose Street, was a block on Third Street occupied by the Fred Kemp residence. Before the Kemp family bought that place it was occupied by the Hollenbeck family. This building was erected in the early days of San Juan.

In 1856 the next block was vacant, but afterwards a livery stable was built on it by T. J. McKnight. He also built a residence on it, which residence is now occupied by Mark Regan. McKnight sold the property to Clarence Bowman who, in turn, sold it to Mark Regan.

Crossing San Jose Street we come to the block on Third Street, between San Jose and Tuolumne Streets. The first house on this block was that occupied by Tom Clark whose wife was one of the Donner party. Clark subsequently sold the place to a man by the name of Reynolds, who was in the sheep business.

The first house that I remember being on Third Street, between Tuolumne and Monterey Streets, was that of Dr. Simmons.

The block between Monterey and Church streets and Second and Third Streets was owned by John Birmingham, a veteran of the Mexican war and afterwards justice of the peace. Mr. Birmingham was a first-class carpenter. On this tract of land he afterwards built a two-story house. Birmingham had a son by the name of Alec who met with an untimely death owing to an accidental pistol shot, whilst he and "CC" Zanetta were returning from a business trip to Hollister.

On North Street, between Second and Third Streets, was a piece of land that was, at this time, owned and occupied by a Mexican. This Mexican afterwards sold this piece of land to Chas. Sherwood, my son-in-law's father.

The Sherwood family occupied the place for years and still own the property. Mr. and Mrs. Sherwood died within one day of each other, and were buried on the same day.

Ernie, or as he is familiarly known in Watsonville, "Shorty" Sherwood (my son-in-law) has been for years a trusted employee of the Chas. Ford Company. He is a popular member of the Elks, the Eagles, and Native Sons.

Retracing our steps to the west side of Third Street and in taking up the homes along that thoroughfare from the Bowie residence, we first come to an old, very old, frame structure that from time to time had different occupants, Americans, Mexicans and other nationalities.

On the same side, across Mokelumne Street on the next block between Mokelumne and Polk Streets, was the residence of Daniel Harris, a merchant.

In the same block, further on, was the residence of Refugio Cheverria,[10] a vaquero widely known throughout that section; and as square and honest a man as ever lived. In after years he worked for a long time for the Flint, Bixby Co.

In the next block there was another small dwelling that was occupied by Bob Rowls, one of the overland stage drivers.

Adjoining the Rowls home, on Third Street, was a residence occupied by Madame Pilar, an old Spanish mid-wife.

The next house on that same block was occupied by Jas. Stanley, a harness maker.

In the next block, between Monterey and Tuolumne Streets, and Third and Fourth Streets, there was only one house. This house was occupied by Caleb Brummett, father of

Harwell Brummett, the newspaper editor, who, on the court-house steps, at Hollister, years afterwards, was killed by Carlton, a rival editor.

I do not remember who lived on the next block, but it was subsequently purchased by Fielding Hodges who still lives there.

The next block, further on, only contained one residence. It was occupied by the Hodges family, that is, Fielding Hodges' parents.   It was afterward occupied by Frank Black and family early settlers of San Juan.

Taking in Fourth Street, at the corner of Monterey and Fourth streets the Chalmer's place was located. The Chalmer's holding was a large piece of land known as lot 8 on the official map.   George Chalmer's residence was built some distance from Fourth Street, well onto the hill, This structure was burned down but was rebuilt.

Adjoining the Chalmer's place, on the west side of Fourth Street, was the Hall place.

Next to the Hall place, on the same side of Fourth Street, came the Bowman place.

Adjacent to the Bowman place came the old adobe residence of Borondo, and then there were several other adobe buildings, some of which were said to be occupied at various times, in the upper stories, by bandits, both Mexican and American, who, hid therein, slept by day, and prowled around during the night.

The blocks fronting on the east side of Fourth Street were vacant.

Coming into town from the north, the first thoroughfare the traveler traversed was First Street.   First Street is the street that the present school is on.[11] It extended from' away out to the limits of the city, on what might be called the highway, and ran from the north towards the north end of the old mission building, where it stopped.

The traveler, coming to San Juan, from the north, as we have said before, came in on First Street, as far as Monterey Street, and generally, turned to the right and took either Second or Third Street for further progress.

Coming from the north on the right-hand side of the road the first residence thereon was John Bigley's family home. Bigley was an early settler in San Juan and married one of the Smith girls. The Smith family came to California in 1849. Bigley followed teaming, with a four-horse team, between Alviso and San Juan. In those days of long extended credit, Bigley was known as a rather peculiar man, inasmuch as he never ran a bill—paid cash for what he wanted and demanded cash in return for his labors.

This matter of extended credit was a time-honored custom in the early days and this same custom proved the undoing of the early Californians. They would run a bill, then a note or a mortgage on their land was given, after which came the inevitable result, their landed possessions were taken from them.

"Jack" Bigley, as he was familiarly known, had another peculiar characteristic—he never had a seat on his wagon. He either rode on the footboard or walked alongside his team. Generally he stood up and drove. Many a time have I seen "Jack" Bigley come in from Alviso in the depth of winter, bare-footed, with his pants rolled up to his knees.

Crossing over from Bigley's place to the left of First Street the first home was that of Andrew (Andy) Abbe. Mr. Abbe, after he left his home on the San Justo grant, moved north of town on a ten acre tract or more and set out the first orchard that the San Juan Valley boasted of. He also, at the same time built a home on this piece of land. His family, a large one, was born and raised in this home. Andy Abbe was a pleasant, jovial man, always meeting everyone with a smile and a laugh and was always ready to exchange repartee with you. He was a busy man; when not teaming he was engaged in working on the county roads. He served as road supervisor of that district for years.

ROSCOE HODGDON'S FINAL RESTING PLACE. BELL CIRCA 1880

CHAPTER IX

Road Supervisors had little money to do road-work with—
Hodgdon who had the fire bell placed on his grave—
The killing of Andrew Barker

IT WILL BE remembered that at that time there was imposed upon all citizens a two dollar school poll tax and a road poll tax. The citizens could get out of paying cash on the road poll tax by working on the roads. Accordingly, one can well imagine what sort of work and how much work could be gotten out of a party of citizens whiling away their time on the roads to save the two dollar poll tax. The wage, in those days, was two dollars per day. There was very little road money to be secured and the roads were extremely bad; muddy in winter, mud so thick and heavy that you could not get through it with the team; and, in the summer, two or three inches of stifling dust.

Mr. Abbe, as the road supervisor, was the recipient of many kicks and complaints regarding the condition of the roads. He always met these growls with patience, and did the best he could on the roads with the meager pittance allowed him by the county. I doubt that Mr. Abbe had enough money at one time to properly condition a single mile of road.

He had four sons: Frank, who after his graduation from school, taught school in San Juan. (This son possesses the distinction of being the only school-teacher in the U. S. A., who graduated, a full-fledged printer, in two weeks from the weekly Free Lance office, in Hollister, when it was conducted by W. B. Winn. Frank says his rapidity in learning the printing trade was due to his splendid foreman, one Jas. G. Piratsky).

George, Charles and Fred Abbe were Andrew Abbe's other sons. Charles lives somewhere on the San Benito river on his ranch, and Frank, George and Fred now constitute the Abbe firm of San Juan, which conducts one of the largest general merchandise stores in San Benito county. Frank Abbe founded the Abbe Company after he retired from teaching school.

Andrew Abbe had several daughters. One of these daughters married E. A. Pierce who had settled in the San Juan Canyon, and had a beautiful home there. The youngest daughter married the son of San Juan's pioneer hotel man, Angelo Zanetta.

Next to the Abbe home, on the left-hand side of First Street, was the home of Vick McGarvey who, for many years, was assessor of Monterey county. McGarvey had quite an extended tract of land well down the hill.

Let me remark right here that San Juan occupies the unique position of being on an elevation from which water runs down on all sides. You can't call it a hill on which the town is located. It seems to me to be rather a throw-off from the surrounding hills in order to make one of the prettiest sites imaginable for a town.

After Mr. McGarvey sold his place it was occupied by Chas. Goodrich, Greg Sanchez and others. In 1868 part of the land was bought for school purposes.

Next to the McGarvey home, part of which was sold, for school purposes, there was a large vacant place which was also eventually acquired by the school district. This property, in the early days, was built on by W. G. Hubbard. The place was afterwards occupied by Arthur Graham, who married Fanny Canfield. Mr. Graham, later, ran a butcher shop in San Juan. He was also a member of the San Juan fire department, and, at one time, ran the Plaza Hotel. Mr. and Mrs. Graham died in their San Juan home within a day of each other, both dying from typhoid pneumonia.

Next to the Graham home was the home of Sam Clark.

Somewhere along that side of the street there lived, at one time, Bill Burnett, afterwards known as the only sheriff of San Benito county that ever made money out of the office.

I think Morris Sullivan also lived in one of the houses along that side of the street.

Well back from First Street on the left hand side, lived Jas. Emmons. There was an old building attached to Emmons' place, it was there before my family moved to San Juan and whilst it was occupied by many people and families I can not now recall their names.

Next to Emmons' place came the residence of Judge Jas. F. Breen, who served several years as superior judge of San Benito county. Judge Breen's home on this tract was a very large, commodious and handsome structure. It was built for him by Con Hickey, when Judge Breen married Jas. McMahon's daughter Kate.

Judge Breen owned, down in the river bottom, some two hundred acres of land which eventually he set out to pears.

After the Breen's property there was no further habitation and First Street terminated at a fence attached to the corner of the mission building.

Retracing our steps across First Street, after the Bigley home, coming towards town, there was a vacant lot. Eventually this lot was built on by Chas. Mitchell, a brother-in-law of Dr. Thomas Flint.

On the block between First, Second, North and Church Streets there was a building that was erected by John Hunt, somewhere around 1858-1859.

Hunt was a blacksmith and had a shop there, but he did not stay in San Juan long.

Mrs. Nidever, a widow, occupied the Hunt place for a long time afterwards.

There were no more buildings on the right hand side of First Street up to its termination against the mission building.

We now take up Second Street from its beginning. North, on the west side of Second Street, between North and Church Streets, there was a building occupied by Major McMichael. It was built there somewhere along 1859-60.[12] Mr. McMichael, who purchased the ranch on the road north of town, was a cattle man who had come over to the mission town from the San Joaquin Valley. After living on his ranch for awhile he moved into town and built this home. His wife is still alive and is living on this same place with her daughter, Annie.

Miss McMichael is postmistress of San Juan, having been appointed to that office during the administration of Cleveland, and notwithstanding the changes of presidents no one has ever attempted to displace her. At one time, during a Republican administration, a San Juanite intimated that he would like to be appointed to the office, but Hon. Thos. Flint, Jr., who at that time was one of the leading Republicans in the State, emphatically said "no" to such a proposition, and Miss McMichael remained undisturbed. She still holds the office, giving excellent service, and she is universally beloved.

On the west side of Second Street, on the corner of Church Street there was a church building in the later '50's. This church belonged to the Methodist Church South.

On the east side of Second Street, on the corner of Monterey Street was a residence, in the early '50's, which was occupied by a family by the name of Moore. This was in 1855 or 1856.

On the same side of Second Street, on the southeast corner of Tuolumne and Second Streets, there was a residence occupied by W. E. Lovett.

Continuing further on the same side of Second Street on the southeast corner of Jefferson and Second Streets, there was a residence occupied by the Edmondson family. Mr. Edmondson was a cattle man who settled there but did not remain in San Juan long. He sold this property afterwards to W. G. Hubbard, a blacksmith.

Edmondson owned the east half of the block, and on the west half of the same block there resided John Silk and Roscoe Hodgdon.   The latter conducted a carpenter shop in San Juan.

Mr. Hodgdon was a member of the fire department.   The fire department at one time bought a bell and this bell was left on the front porch of Mr. Hodgdon's residence.   Unfortunately Hodgdon used to go on "periodicals" and one night coming home late, in a spirit of exhiliration, he struck the bell with a hand-axe and the impact broke the bell.   The firemen were justly indignant, and at a called meeting it was moved and carried that Mr. Hodgdon pay for the bell.

Hodgdon did so and announced that as the bell was his he wanted it placed at the head of his grave.   At his burial the firemen placed the coffin on the fire truck and with a band of music playing a burial dirge proceeded to the cemetery.   So, if any of my readers desire to view the last resting place of Roscoe Hodgdon they can find it easily by noting the bell at the head of a certain grave in the cemetery on the road to "The Rocks," outside of San Juan.

Between Jefferson and San Jose Streets, on the west side of Second Street, there formerly was an old barn.   The east side of this block was occupied by Hubbard's blacksmith shop. Hubbard's blacksmith shop was quite an institution in those days.   I remember, it had, at one time, three fires running, day after day.   It also comprised a carriage making and paint shop.

The paint shop was run by Jack Nagel, who was hired by Hubbard.   Nagel was a very fine artist, or, I should say, mechanic, in his line.   He was afterwards employed by the Overland Stage Company to keep its stages freshly painted and neat looking.

All iron work was forged by hand and dressed in a vise with files, being fashioned for fine buggies, spring wagons and freight wagons.   Horseshoes were also forged.   The blacksmith would cut up a piece of iron, turn it into a shoe on the anvil, cut a groove in it and punch the nail holes in it. Nails were bought then but they all had to be pointed by hand. Usually two men, or helpers as they were called, assisted with sledge hammers in the shaping.

It was in front of this shop, on Second Street, that the old plaza cannon was blown up.

One of Hubbard's employes, a blacksmith, had an argument the night before with a companion, and the argument took a turn involving the question of whether or not the old cannon could be "busted." Hubbard's employe claimed it could, and so the next morning early (about five o'clock) he put in an extra heavy charge and plugged the cannon with sand. After getting the cannon properly prepared for the "bust-up," the man took a long stick and attaching his lighted cigar to the end of it, stood off some distance and touched the glowing end of the cigar to the vent hole. The man remembered no more for some time for the concussion of the cannon knocked him northeast by southwest, and it was about twenty minutes before he came to and inquired, "Where was I?" No one could answer the question.

A piece of this cannon went through the roof of the residence of Jas. McMahon, over two blocks away, tearing a big hole in the roof. Pieces of the cannon were picked up all over town, in fact, it was smashed to smithereens. Strange to relate, however, the man was uninjured.

After that we had to use anvils for our celebrations—the old cannon was a thing of the past.

On the opposite side of Second Street, on the corner of Second and San Jose Streets, John Geaster built the National Hotel in 1858. It was a three-story building. The upper story, being drawn in closer than the main building, made the top story somewhat narrower. For that reason it was made into a hall. This hall was used as a lodge room for Texas Lodge, F. & A. M. The reason the San Juan Bautista Masons adopted the name "Texas," I am told, was due to the fact that the majority of the members comprising the lodge were from Texas.

Downstairs there was a large bar and billiard room on one side, with a hall above for dancing and small shows. Off from this hall was the dining room and wash room. The wash room had in it a long sink, with tin basins and roller towels. The bedrooms were small with a commode, a wash bowl, pitcher for water, a towel and perhaps one or two chairs. In some of the rooms there was a small stand whereon to place a candle-stick containing a candle.

There were no toilets or bathrooms in those days. Bathing was a somewhat lost art. It was remarked about several prominent citizens that they went without a bath for a year.

Across San Jose Street on the corner of Second and San Jose Streets, there was a long wooden building which, in my early recollection of San Juan, was occupied as a merchandise store, it being conducted by a man by the name of Strode. It had been used, originally, as a school-house and then the post-office was installed there, in fact, the building had been used for many purposes. In after years, until 1863, it was run as a saloon, when Fred Kemp bought it from Bill Arnold. Bill Arnold was afterwards shot and killed in the Temple Saloon, in the Hildreth block, in Watsonville, by Chas. O'Neil.

It was in this saloon, while it was being conducted by Fred Kemp, that Vic McGarvey shot and killed Andrew Barker. Andrew Barker resided on a lot on the north end of Third Street. He had accumulated about $5,000 which he had buried in the yard of his home. One day after an extended absence from home, he went to look at his buried treasure and found it gone. He was wild over his loss. He had an Indian woman working for him in the house and in his rage he went so far as to hang her in order to make her confess to the theft. She knew nothing about it, and after torturing the woman he cut her down and released her.

Barker went to San Francisco and consulted a medium. The soothsayer told him the money was taken by a light-haired man who lived within sight of his home. Vic McGarvey lived on First Street on rather high ground, and having light hair, answered the description given by the medium. When Barker returned he accused McGarvey of taking his money. He swore he would kill McGarvey, on sight, the next time that they met. Barker was always armed with a pistol and bowie knife. He had a violent temper, and was very quarrelsome at all times, especially if under the influence of liquor. He was a civil engineer.

McGarvey, instead of going home to get a pistol, went to Monsieur Durin, a nearby French gunsmith, and borrowed a shotgun and had Durin load the weapon with powder and buckshot, telling the gunsmith he desired the loan of the gun to kill some wild animals. Putting the gun on his shoulder he went straight to Kemp's saloon. As he entered he saw Barker opposite the door, seated in a chair apparently reading a newspaper, but in reality looking over its top, watching the door.

McGarvey said, "I am armed! Defend yourself!"

As Barker arose, McGarvey shot him, the buckshot penetrating Barker's breast, when Barker, after receiving the shot, partially turned around, McGarvey let him have the other loaded barrel of the gun in the back. Barker was killed instantly.

McGarvey was tried for the killing and was acquitted.

Sometime afterwards there was a story current to the effect that it was Barker's wife that dug up the money and hid it in another place, fearing that Barker's cache might be discovered by some thief. When Barker discovered his loss and got into such a rage over it, fearing that he would kill her, his wife remained silent. I cannot vouch for the authenticity of this story.

Fred Kemp was a very fine man.   He was quiet and un-assuming, and treated everyone alike.   His saloon was more like a club than a barroom.   All of the best men in the district would repair there to enjoy an evening or talk over business to-gether.   It did not matter who they were, from governor to constable or commanding officer to low private, at some time or another they would all be found at Kemp's saloon.   Farmers would congregate to talk about their crops; cattle and sheep men always were to be found there discussing their flocks and pros-pects.   There was never any rowdyism allowed about the place. Kemp never encouraged the buying of liquor and was never known to sit in on a game of cards.   He always had a kind word for everyone.   His hospitality was known far and wide. A staunch Democrat, he never talked politics, and accordingly Republicans and Democrats, alike, would make his saloon their headquarters.   No one could ever say that Fred Kemp got a nickel dishonestly.

He lived in the same block on which his saloon was lo-cated.   His store-house was always well filled, as he bought goods in San Francisco, wholesale.

A stranger arriving in town and inquiring for certain parties would be immediately told to "go down to Fred Kemp's saloon and ask Fred about them.   He will tell you where they are to be found!"

His wife is still alive and is still living in the old home with her son, Fred, who is now county supervisor of the San Juan district.   Fred has built many dwellings on the block and is a very enterprising young man.

On the east side of Second Street, across from Kemp's on the corner of San Jose and Second Street, was the Church building bought by Leon Bullier and occupied by him as a dwelling and barber shop.

MASONIC BUILDING BUILT 1868

CHAPTER X

*Some noted characters that lived in San Juan in the early days
—Luis Chavez, the bandit—The great rainfall in
1862—The San Juan Canyon*

EXT TO this place, east, on Second Street, was Victor Jerbet's place. Mr. Jerbet had a small vineyard of three or four acres and made both red and white wine. He had a small saloon in the front of his place where he retailed the products of his vineyard.

Then came the mission church property which extended up to the plaza. The church owned seventeen acres which embraced not only the land on which the church was located, but eleven or twelve acres of an orchard on the river bench below.

On the west side of Second street, between Mokelumne and Polk Streets, on the corner of Polk and Second Streets, was located the residence of Jas. McMahon.

The Masonic building, on the corner of Mokelumne and Second Streets, was erected years later.[13]

On the west side of Second street, between Mariposa and Polk streets, was the home of the Carreagas, a noted Spanish family in San Juan's early days.

On the corner of Second and Mariposa streets there was erected a wooden building in which was conducted a drug store, stationery store, postoffice, express office and a telegraph office—they were all combined in the one business enterprise. The store was conducted by Thos. Magner, who married into the Carreaga family. The store, was run by different ones in the same line of endeavor one of whom was R. H. Brotherton. "Bob," as he was familiarly known, was one of the finest looking men I ever saw. In those days there was no such title bestowed upon anyone as "Mr." It was Bob, Henry, Frank, or John, as the case might be. "Bob" Brotherton was not only a first-class druggist but an expert telegrapher as well. He was a man who possessed a fine education.

I remember an incident in which he figured.

At one time the cattle on the plains of the San Joaquin Valley were quite numerous and they had a habit of alleviating their itchiness by rubbing their sides against the telegraph poles. Owing to the constant repetition of this rubbing a number of these poles were laid low. Brotherton was notified by the head office, in San Francisco, of the condition of affairs, and asked to repair the line between San Juan and Visalia. Visalia is one of the oldest towns in the San Joaquin Valley.

Brotherton, starting out on his journey, could find no one to help him. Finally, on the other side of the Pacheco Pass, he fell in with a number of vaqueros and by liberally supplying them with liquor, got them to consent to go with him. They did so and Brotherton repaired the line in short order. When Brotherton sent in his bill for the work, there was an item thereon in which "refreshments" were charged some forty or fifty dollars. The head office could not make out how any man could get away with forty or fifty dollars' worth of refreshments, and so "Bob" was summoned to San Francisco to explain. "Bob" told the hi-muck-a-mucks that "refreshments" stood for liquor that he had supplied his employes with in order to retain their services. The magnates went up in the air and when they came down, told "Bob" that henceforth, and hereafter, under no circumstances to ever itemize liquor on a bill as "refreshments." To always be sure and call it "hardware!"

Brotherton married Miss Lucy Canfield, of the Canfield family, and subsequently taught school, and whilst teaching school he studied law and was graduated, and became one of the leading lawyers in the state. He, at one time, practiced law in Hollister. I remember that he was considered an authority, even the late Hon. M. T. Dooling, judge of the federal court, and N. C. Briggs, another leading Hollister attorney, after cogitating over a certain law point decided to go to "Bob" Brotherton and ask him about it.

Poor "Bob," his last days were truly pitiful, as a disease that afflicted him made him, indeed, a miserable object. Many regrets were expressed at his death, for everyone who knew him admired his brilliancy and learning.

Adjoining this drug store, on the west on Second street, was a residence occupied by Pedro Carlos. Carlos was the son-in-law of Manuel Larios. He was a barber and had a shop in the same building in which he resided. He, at one time, owned a home on an elevation on the road to Sargent station known as the McKee place. It is still in the possession of some of the McKee heirs.

Pedro Carlos will go down into history as the inventor of the card game "pedro." He, in his leisure moments, would derive great pleasure from card playing and finally he evolved the game of pedro, which game is now played throughout the United States. But few people realize that pedro was invented in San Juan.

Another game popular in early days, in San Juan, was pitch seven up. Carlos enlarged this game by adding the five spot of trumps.

On Mariposa street the thoroughfare runs down alongside of the Plaza Hotel and between Second and Third Streets was a two-story residence building owned by the Carreagas.

The two Carreaga brothers, Juan and Ramon, owned, at one time, six-hundred acres across the San Benito river between the Sanchez grant and the San Justo grant. This land is now owned by the heirs of Patrick Breen.

One of the Carreaga boys married a daughter of Buenaventura, the latter was a Frenchman and was married to a Borondo. He came to San Juan in the early days, was a cobbler by trade, and lived on Fourth street on a place embracing four or five acres, which extended along Washington street. He had a small vineyard on this place.

After the Carreaga boys, Juan and Ramon, disposed of their property in and near San Juan, they moved to Santa Maria and at that place became very wealthy; oil eventually being discovered on the lands that they owned there.

We have remarked, heretofore, that Andrew Abbe had a great deal to do with looking after the roads and streets in that district. While engaged in leveling off Second street his plow turned up forty or fifty dollars in old Mexican coins. Some of them dating back to 1600. They were all sold at a big premium as they were valuable as keepsakes and souvenirs.

This is all that I remember of the buildings that were scattered here and there in the early days, throughout what is known as San Juan Bautista Mission.

At this point it occurs to me to mention some of the noted characters that I remember in those early days. One was a Mexican by the name of Morales. He was a splendid musician and excelled on the violin; with the guitar to accompany him he furnished all the dance music for the fiestas and dances in that section. He was a general favorite with everybody. No one could surpass the dance music that he gave. Morales' trade was the manufacture of spurs and bridle-bits, and in that line he had no rival. He always turned out first-class work. He was an expert at inlaying spurs and bridle-bits with silver.

Another character that I remember was Ramon Cheverria, a bronco buster. There was no horse that was too wild for Ramon to tackle. He was the one always selected to ride the wild bull at the annual June 24th fiesta, each year. He became a first-class billiardist and it took an expert handler of a billiard cue to defeat him.

Recollection brings back to me another character whom I forgot to mention in going along Third Street in my "ramblings." This was Mondregon, a Spaniard, who kept a store on

the east side of Third Street near Bowie's bakery.   He was
a saddle-maker and could make, out of leather, any article re-
quired by horsemen.   In his line, he too, was an expert, and
as such was known far and wide throughout the state.   He
carried a stock of Mexican saddles, bridles, lariats and quirts.

Let me interject right here that Byrd Harris was the first
child born in San Juan, of American parents.   This is in response to a query made some time ago.

At the end of "The Alameda," going toward home, on
the right, there was, then, a wooden building built of split
redwood in 1855.   This building and land was afterwards
acquired by Sylvester Wilcox.   After buying this building Wilcox repaired it and lived there with his wife, until they both
died.   Part of the old building may be seen there yet.   They
left the property to their son and daughter, Joseph and Adi
Wilcox, who still occupy the place.

Opposite this holding, across the road, was another small
building, similarly constructed, occupied by a Frenchman whose
name I cannot remember.   This Frenchman had a vegetable
garden there.

At the forks of the present road, going to Hollister and
Salinas there lived, in a small house, Rafael Hernandez and his
wife.   Mrs. Hernandez was an Albino, white-haired and near-
sighted.   She was a passionate lover of flowers and had the
prettiest flower garden in that section.   The place was enclosed
by a high picket fence.   I longingly looked at these flowers,
many a time, going and coming from school, but looks availed
me nothing, for Mrs. Hernandez guarded her floral treasures
with vigilance.   She never gave me a single flower although
I longed so much for them.   Rafael Hernandez was a vaquero
of the old school, and in after years was a rider for the Flint,
Bixby Co., on the range.

Opposite the Hernandez place, in a low crudely constructed
habitation, dwelt the Chavez family.   One of Chavez' sons

became the notorious Chavez, a member of the Vasquez robber band, and was killed, towards the close of Vasquez' career, in southern California.

At the turn, the road ran across the creek, which was parallel to the present Hollister place. The water from this creek came from the San Juan canyon, and in the year 1862 this creek overflowed. This overflow deposited an immense number of willow plants which afterwards caused my father much labor and expense to grub out. The creek ran up to the main road that went directly east.

On the road, leading up to the canyon, there was a large two-story adobe house. Part of this building had been used as an old Spanish mill, the mill stones are there yet. I do not remember who built it or occupied it first, but at the time that I am talking about (1855-1860) this adobe was occupied by Lorenzo Twitchell, son of Joshua Twitchell, the man from whom my father bought our place.

On the road towards my father's place, on the west side, there was a building right next to the road occupied by William Stingley. Stingley, in partnership with my father, bought that place from Joshua Twitchell, great-grandfather of Doctor A. R. Lawn, the chiropractor, now practicing his profession in Watsonville.

Afterwards my father and Stingley divided the land—my father taking the land on the east of the line, one hundred and fifty-five acres, and Stingley took the western portion. Subsequently, in some sort of a trade, Joshua Twitchell acquired the Stingley property and lived there for years.

In later years Stingley was killed by being struck by a redwood tree, whilst working under the foremanship of the late ex-supervisor Jas. A. Linscott, of Santa Cruz county, at the Game-Cock lumber camp, above Corralitos.

As years passed the various bends in the road were straightened out and the road was fixed up so as to connect with the

San Juan canyon road.   There was no road to Monterey from this direction.   This road, that I have just described in its entirety, is the road that I traversed going to school.

We will now take in the San Juan canyon road.   Let me here remark that the San Juan canyon, in the early days, was one of the most picturesque spots in that section, and today it is worth anyone's time to visit this truly sylvan retreat, although, to a large extent, its beauty has been somewhat marred by the development made in the canyon by the San Juan Cement Company.[14]

Proceeding up the canyon, from San Juan, the first house that you encountered was a large adobe, now gone.   It has utterly disappeared and yet, at that time, it was one of the landmarks in that vicinity.   Who erected this adobe dwelling I do not know, it looked to me as though the land had been taken up as government land, the building erected and then both building and claim were abandoned.   However, when I knew it, this residence was occupied by Captain Taylor, father of Bartlett Taylor, and his wife.   The Bartlett Taylor, whom in another part of this narrative I chronicled as being shot in Louis Raggio's saloon.

The next house, going up the canyon, was occupied by the family of William Harris, the first school teacher in San Juan.   I was, for awhile, one of Mr. Harris' pupils.   He died at Stockton several years later.

Close to William Harris' residence was another home occupied by Mr. Harris' father and mother.   The Harris family were very fine people.

Proceeding on, the next place one would come to was the home of a man by the name of Quinn.   Old residents in those days used to call the place he occupied, Quinn canyon.

Beyond the Quinn home there was a place occupied by some cattle men, I have forgotten their names, but ultimately their holdings were acquired by Jasper Twitchell, son of old man Joshua Twitchell. Mr. Twitchell built a commodious house there as he had a large family. He beautified the place greatly. It will be remembered that we spoke of Mr. Twitchell as having a business in San Juan. He was a very competent wood worker.

Ultimately, when Jesse D. Carr got his land grant from the government, he ran his survey down one mile wide, so far that it took in all the land embraced in the canyon including some of the Flint, Bixby land, and made it necessary for Flint and other property owners, in that canyon, to buy their land over again from Jesse D. Carr. It is hardly necessary to remark that some hard feelings were stored up against the aforesaid Jesse D. Carr.

Retracing our steps to the old adobe that I mentioned and which has since disappeared: Below this adobe, in the bed of the creek, some hundred years before, the padres had constructed a dam and by means of a ditch leading around the side of the hill, brought the water down onto a flat near San Juan. At the present time San Juan is supplied by a water system from a dam constructed a short distance above the site of this old dam. The original dam was rudely constructed of logs thrown across the bed of the creek in a criss-cross fashion, and filled in with adobe which, when dried, was almost impenetrable. Old residents described the dam to me as being a very good piece of work. However, the big flood in 1862 washed the remainder of this dam out, and all traces of it have disappeared. Its former site today is not easily found.

The water from this dam, when brought into town, in the early days, was conducted to a place where was made the adobe tiles, and in time this water made a big lake there. I remember often witnessing the drivers of the overland stages, after discharging their passengers and before getting ready to stable their horses for the night, driving their animals and the stages through this lake, thereby giving both animals and vehicle a well deserved washing.

Near the old adobe there was, in the early days, a tunnel that ran into the Gabilan range. The tunnel was not run in very far and its site has long since been obliterated. The purpose for which this tunnel was driven into the mountain could never be ascertained.

In those days horse stealing was a common offense. The Indians had no scruples about taking someone's horses, consequently, horse owners, in those days, built large corrals made of adobe, surrounded by a ten or twelve foot wall, in order to keep the thieving marauders out. In this old adobe that I have previously described there was, at the time I am speaking of, the remains of an immense stockade of this description behind the structure.

KEMP SALOON, "THE BOLA DE ORO," BUILT CIRCA 1850

CHAPTER XI

The mysterious killing of a man named Kelly, near Gilroy—
Vasquez, the bandit, comes to the front—The tragedy
at Paicines—Snyder's account of the raid

RIGHT HERE recollection brings back to me a strange and mysterious killing that occurred near Gilroy. This occurred in 1870. A woman by the name of Mrs. Page came, via stage, from Watsonville to Gilroy. On arriving at the latter place she hired a horse and buggy and started toward San Juan, passing the Miller-Bloomfield ranch, where an employe named Kelly was employed. She asked Kelly to take a ride with her and he accepted. There was a cluster of willows on the side of the road between Miller's home and the Sargent place. The woman invited Kelly to take a walk with her, at this point, and about two hundred yards from the road she drew a pistol and shot him through his head, and also through his heart, killing him instantly. She left him lying there and rode back to Gilroy and gave herself up to the authorities. At the preliminary examination Mrs. Page testified that the reason that she killed Kelly was that he had slandered her. She wanted him to retract the slander, he refused, and she killed him.

The outcome of this case I do not remember but it was a big sensation in this section of the state for a long time on account of the woman having announced her destination as San Juan, when she hired the buggy. All of San Juan turned out, en masse, to see if they knew her. But she was never identified.

At this point I wish to digress and take up the career of one of California's celebrated bandits, who certainly deserves more than a passing notice. I allude to Tiburcio Vasquez, who, in 1873, was committing depredations throughout Monterey, Santa Clara and counties south.   Vasquez will go down in the annals of California crime alongside of Joaquin Murietta, California's bandit king, in the fifties.

Vasquez, for awhile, was a very striking figure in the criminal records of the state, and the press was full of his exploits.   Inasmuch as he was well known in San Juan and frequently came there, accompanied by some of his confederates, one of whom was Chavez, mentioned elsewhere as being one of my schoolmates, at San Juan, I think it might be of interest to the readers of these memoirs that I here insert something regarding this man.

Vasquez was sent, from Los Angeles county in 1857, to the penitentiary for horse stealing.   He escaped from that prison but was soon captured and was imprisoned until 1863.

After he was released he joined forces with two worthies by the name of Procopio and Soto—two notorious hombres, These two men, Procopio and Soto, were known far and wide as desperate men.   Sheriff Harry Morse, of Alameda, was on the hunt for Soto to answer for some crime he had committed.   The two men met and in the gun-fight that ensued Soto was killed.

Vasquez then organized an augmented band of desperadoes and made a raid on Paicines, San Benito County, which I will give in full as the tragedy was related by Mr. A. Snyder, the keeper of the store that was raided at Paicines.

"About five o'clock p. m., of August 26, 1873, Adone Levia and Juan Gonzales came into my store, as they had done at other times, and bought and paid for some merchandise. They hung around the store until about sundown at which time Wm. Burnett, driver of the New Idria stage arrived.   Being a half an hour earlier than usual that evening I changed the mail and stepped outside to see the stage off.   In five or six minutes after the stage had left for New Idria, Vasquez, Morina and Chavez appeared in front of the store on horses. They were armed with revolvers and rifles.   They alighted from their horses and tied them to the fence close up to my store porch. I watched them closely as they were more heavily armed than at other times when they purchased and paid for goods. I noticed, while they were tying their horses, that Chavez had a lot of rope in his side coat pockets. They eyed me very closely while tying up their horses.

"Mr. Lewis Smith, a neighbor, just then came up and stepped into the store and called for a broom. I told him I did not like the looks of those fellows outside. In a moment the three men came in, Vasquez inquiring for a letter by some Spanish name. I stepped behind the desk to look for the letter called for and at the same time I heard someone say in an audible voice, 'Lay down! lay down!' Finding no mail for the name called for I turned to tell them so, when I saw my clerk, John Uzuruth, and Lewis Smith and Henry Murray lying on the floor.

"Across the room from me stood Gonzales and Don Levia with six-shooters aimed at me, and Morina, standing in the door with a rifle pointed at me, ordering me to lie down, but I would not do so at first. My first impulse was to shoot with a rifle which I had nearby, but it had but one load and I thought of my family in an adjoining building. If I should shoot one of the men I would be killed anyway, and possibly my family, also.

They spoke with vehemence and said that they would blow the top of my head off, drawing a bead on me at the same time. I need not tell how large those cylinders looked to me at that moment, but, I will say that they seemed to grow larger every moment. I submitted and laid down behind my desk. I will say it was the most trying thing I had ever done in my life but it was to save my own life and that of my family that I submitted. Vasquez tied my hands behind my back, laid me on my face and covered me with a blanket. They tied my clerk's hands behind his back and then tied his feet to his hands and laid him on his face. They tied Mr. Smith and Mr. Murray the same way.

"Vasquez then remarked, 'Boys, I am sorry to treat you this way!' But if I should try to make my living by honest work and the people should find out who I am, they would hang me inside of a week! The only way I have to make a living is robbing other people, and, as long as they have money, I am going to have my share!' He also told me that he would spare my life as I had submitted. They then commenced to pilfer the store and our pockets.

"About this time I heard Mr. Haley, who drove a four-horse team, calling my name. I dared not answer. The bandits hit him on the head with a six-shooter, took him off the wagon and tied him to the front wheel. They took all the money he had and left him in that condition. He worked himself loose but he still stood stooped over that way for fear that they would find he was untied.

"By this time Mr. Connolly and his wife and boy came along. They were stopped and Mr. Connolly was brought near the store and tied, then laid on the ground. Mrs. Connolly screamed at the top of her voice and they threatened to shoot her as they were afraid she would alarm the neighbors. Mrs. Snyder came out and took her by the hand and led her into the house telling her to be quiet and maybe their lives would be spared. The Connolly boy crawled across the road on his hands and knees, climbed a fence and crossed the river to a neighbor.

"The hostler at the barn was told to lie down, but not knowing what it meant laughed. They hit him on the head with a gun, tied him up and took him behind the barn.

"George Redford of Gilroy, with a four-horse team, drove up and started to unhitch his team. They ordered him to lie down. He was hard of hearing and ran once around his wagon and then into the stable where they shot him through the heart.

"A Frenchman who had stopped here with a band of sheep for the night knew them and they knew him. While nearing the barn they shot at him, tearing his upper teeth out. He jumped the fence into an adjoining field and then ran back on the store porch, they after him. As he was running onto the porch they shot him through the breast. I heard him fall and struggle in death.

"About this time I heard another shot in front of the hotel. Leland Davidson, proprietor of the hotel, who was sick and was not aware of what was going on, heard the shooting and arose from his chair, went to the front door and had opened it partly, when his wife ran in from the rear screaming to her husband to close the door as robbers were looting the store. She reached up over his shoulder to close the door when Vasquez, appearing in front, fired through the door with his rifle. The ball entered Davidson's heart. He fell back in his wife's arms and expired.

"They then came in to where I was laying on the floor," continued Mr. Snyder, "took me to the room where my family was congregated. They ordered Mrs. Snyder to hand over all the money in the house, and she promised them she would if they would spare my life. They agreed to do this.

"After getting all the money there was in the house they took me back to the store. On the way back Chavez and Vasquez held a conversation in Spanish. Vasquez finally told Chavez, in English, that he was captain of this band and he was going to save my life. Taking me to the store they laid me down on my side, my hands tied behind me, and covered me with a blanket, then they commenced packing their horses with goods from the store.

"From being tied so tightly my hands and arms were swollen and pained me terribly. I made a special request for the third time to loosen the ropes. Vasquez examined them, and saying they were too tight slackened them up which was a great relief.

"They helped themselves to sardines, oysters, cheese, and crackers and had a hearty supper. I asked them to hurry as

I was hungry. They said that they were hungry, and would not go until they had finished their lunch. When they had finished Vasquez told them to go to the stable and bring out all of the good horses which they would drive ahead of them. They took eleven horses from the stable, two of them mine, and drove them off. A blind horse they killed.

"I was robbed of about $600 worth of goods, two horses, $430 in coin, my watch and weapons. They got, altogether, from the party, about $1200 in coin.

"When they left we got to our feet. The Smith boy, not being tied, untied his father and Mr. Smith untied the rest of us. I went, at once, to where my family were and they were safe. I next went to Mr. Davidson's room and found him dead and his wife crying. Returning to the store, on the porch, lay the Frenchman, dead. Going to the barn with a lantern I found George Redford lying dead on his face on a bale of hay in a stall.

"The next morning there was a crowd of neighbors there who had heard of the robbing and murders.

"During the shooting Mrs. Snyder and Mrs. Sam Moore had forethought enough to lie flat on the floor to escape the bullets that were flying around."

Thus ends the account of Vasquez' raid on Paicines as narrated by Mr. Snyder. This murderous raid was the sensation of the entire country for weeks after it occurred and it incited renewed efforts to run down and capture Vasquez.

After this startling exploit Vasquez proceeded south and was finally captured in Los Angeles. He was brought back, but San Benito county, not having the facilities for trying him, transferred him to the San Jose jail, and tried him in that county.

He was found guilty and hanged on March 19, 1875.

After Vasquez was hanged at San Jose his chief lieutenant, Chavez, fled to Mexico. Information reached San Juan as to where Chavez was living.   Louis Raggio Jr. started for New Mexico found Chavez and in an attempt to arrest him, killed him. The state had offered a reward of $2,500 for Chavez dead or alive and accordingly his head was severed from his body and brought back to San Juan as proof for the reward.   Raggio put in a claim for the reward and had a great deal of trouble over it. I do not remember whether he got the reward or not.

In 1876 I had a band of sheep pastured in Pleasant Valley, in the Coalinga district, guarded by several sheepherders. At the time there were a great many sheepmen in that district with their flocks. One of these sheep owners was Geo. W. McConnell, afterwards, for years, the assessor of San Benito county. Out of this meeting there grew an acquaintanceship and friendship between McConnell and myself that continued until the death of McConnell.

I suspect that George found his charming wife in the vicinity of the San Benito store.   Her maiden name was Kennedy and she lived, with her folks, on the upper San Benito.   George, driving his flocks to and from the Coalinga and the Panoche sections, formed an acquaintance with Annie Kennedy, and subsequently, they were married.   A most charming woman was Mrs. McConnell, who, with her husband, has long since passed away.

There were remnants of the Vasquez band traveling through that section yet.   They stole horses and cattle. Eventually these men were wiped out.

Where my sheep were pastured in Pleasant Valley was in a direct line with the Cantua canyon, one of Joaquin Murietta's and Tubercio Vasquez' strongholds in their days of banditry. There was another picturesque canyon between where I. was located and the Cholame Valley.   In this canyon there was another band of desperadoes that had been affiliated with Murietta and Vasquez.

I was about three miles from my nearest neighbor.   Somehow or another I escaped.   I was never preyed upon by these desperadoes although they passed my location, coming and going. I, however, always felt nervous over the situation as I did not know what a day or night might bring forth.

One morning, about six or seven o'clock, three of these desperadoes, in a gang, rode up on horseback to my place. Each one of them had a rifle and a six-shooter and a bowie knife in his belt. I was frightened, of course, but I assumed a calm demeanor and asked them to alight and have some breakfast with me. In the corner of the cabin which I occupied, was my shot-gun, loaded with buckshot. I made up my mind that I would use that shot-gun if anything untoward happened. A long table that we used when the sheepherders came to shear the sheep stood between me and the robbers. When I extended the invitation, they dismounted and came into the cabin. Whilst I was cooking the breakfast I kept my eye on them as I did not know what minute trouble would ensue.

I gave the desperadoes a pretty fair breakfast inasmuch as I had my own cow and had plenty of butter and milk and the chickens that I had, furnished me with fresh eggs. The three men ate heartily and, after thanking me for the meal, mounted their steeds and rode away. A short distance from my place they robbed a sheepherder of all the money he had, also his grub.

The situation in that section was too dangerous, and I, with the rest of the sheepmen, in the valley, made up my mind to get out of there as soon as possible. We all did. We left there the ensuing season, which was a dry year. Practically all the sheepmen lost their herds by starvation.

In 1877 one San Juan sheepman, Albion Baker, drove his herd of 8,000 sheep into the high Sierras where there was pasturage. After skirmishing around through that region, he came out in the fall with 1,000 head. He was heavily in debt and turned over the 1,000 head to his creditors.

CHAPTER XII

*How San Juan folks lived in early days—How pioneer mothers
helped their husbands—Grain was taken to grist mill at
Corralitos—My venture into the sheep business.*

OW we lived after we settled near San Juan deserves more than passing notice, and undoubtedly
will prove of interest to those who live in the midst
of comfort and plenty nowadays.

To begin with, we raised practically all that we ate.

In Gentry county, Missouri where, out in the country, we
had lived in a log cabin (I was born in that log cabin), my
mother, when preparing for the trip overland gathered together
packages of different kinds of vegetable seeds—I often wondered, afterwards, where she got so many different varieties. She
also brought along medicinal plants, with which, after we settled in the land of "milk and honey," she doctored the children.

It would be well to interpolate right here that my father,
with three other young fellows,[15] had made the trip across the
plains in 1850, and returned, via the Isthmus, to Missouri after
a short stay in California in 1851. After my father's return he
prepared the family for the trip overland to the Golden State.

He informed my mother of the fertility of California's
soil, its climate and many other items that guided her in making her selection of seeds, etc. Therefore, during our first years
in the San Juan Valley, we had all the vegetables we could
eat and then some.

When my father bought the place, on the outskirts of San
Juan, included in the purchase price were a few hogs, and so,
with the pork occasionally, we had plenty of our own meat.
The tea, sugar, coffee, soap and candles we bought from the
village merchants. This was not for long, however, for before a year had passed my mother cut out the purchase of soap

and candles, and made those two articles herself—another il-lustration of the manner in which the pioneer women, who came to this state, arose to the occasion and proved themselves verit-able help-mates to their husbands.   The sugar used then was mostly China sugar, which was put up in fifty pound mats. This sugar could be purchased at the San Juan stores.   The sugar which was somewhat dirty, left nearly always a residue of some sort of sediment in the bottom of the cups, however, we never missed a meal if sugar was lacking.

It was not long before the railroad was constructed across the Isthmus of Panama and then we got New Orleans sugar, a big improvement on what we had, originally.

I always fought for the job of going after the sugar—that is, the New Orleans sugar.   It came in large hogsheads which seemed to me must have weighed a thousand pounds or more. The attraction in this task, for me, was due to the fact that in the center of these hogsheads there was always inserted a piece of sugar cane.   This sugar cane reached to. the bottom of the hogshead.   Now, when the storekeeper sold some of this sugar he invariably cut off a small piece of the sugar cane and gave it to the youngster that came after the sugar.   This was a great at-traction for me for that sugar cane was seemingly the sweetest and most luscious thing that I ever tasted.

It was the custom in those days that when the children were sent to a store to make a purchase the child should receive a "pelon" or a "pelon cita" which, in the Spanish, meant a present.   Consequently, the youngsters would either get a piece of candy, a sweet cracker or a slice of the sugar cane, etc.

My father got some seed wheat and sowed a few acres to that cereal.   At that time there were thousands of squirrels on our place, in fact the valley was infested with these rodents. and accordingly we had to commence fighting them in order to keep them from eating the seeds when planted.

In pursuit of these squirrels I developed into a crack run-ner.   I had a Scotch terrier, a great playmate of mine, and if

Mr. Squirrel got any distance from his hole in the ground, barefooted as I was I would, with the assistance of the dog, run him down. My speed in running was due principally to this exercise. Together with the dog, every morning before I went to school, and again when I came home from that institution of learning, I would make the rounds. By closely following this practice we finally scared nearly all the squirrels out of our fields. When the wheat seeded out we would have lost the entire crop had it not been for myself and the dog. After that we fought them with phosphorous and strychnine (we used to procure that mixture at San Jose) and together with shooting and trapping, kept these pests down, but it was years before we finally gained control of them.

In those days there were no machines wherewith to cut grain so we used a reap hook or a cradle. My father got a cradle and cut the standing grain and bound it. There was no way to thresh it, save to tramp it out with horses, Spanish style. We cleaned off a place, flooded it with water, and trampled it over and over again until the sun baked it hard. Around this place my father built a fence with rails. My brother, who was about sixteen, engineered this work. They would bring up a load of bundles of grain, put them in this pen, put the horses inside of the inclosure and then either by riding them or chasing them around would thresh out the grain. The main part of the straw was taken up with forks which were shaken so as to drop any clean grain off of them; then the stalks were thrown over the fence. This process was repeated over and over again until the grain and straw, remaining in the inclosure, was ready to be cleaned. When the wind blew, generally in the afternoon, we would take a shovel and throw the remainder of the straw in the air and the wind would blow the chaff away. In that way we succeeded in getting seed and feed for the chickens.

Some of our neighbors chipped in and got a fan mill. We would borrow this fan mill and, by hard work, would succeed in getting out a ton of grain, and then take this to the mill.

Benjamin Hames had built a grist mill at Corralitos, and we would take this grain over to him to be ground. Hames, it might be well to remark here, was a man who had traveled extensively, had managed several enterprises in Chile and other parts of South America, and was a very well educated man. My brother married his daughter in 1866.

It would take two days to execute this commission. One day to transport the grain over to Corralitos and get it ground, and the next day to retrace our steps to San Juan.

This crop of wheat gave us our own flour which was a more superior article than the flour we got at the store, much of which came from Chile and cost us sixteen dollars a barrel of 196 pounds.

It was while making these trips that I first saw Watsonville. I think it was in 1858 or 1859.

Col. Hollister had a flock of ewes pastured about half a mile from our place. In lambing season the sheep were placed in a corral and at night the young would sometimes lose their mothers in which case the sheepherders would knock the lambs in the head if they could not ascertain to which mother they belonged. I asked Col. Hollister to give me these motherless lambs and he said he would be glad to do so. We had plenty of milk, as we had four or five cows—one of these cows having worked under the yoke whilst crossing the plains. I had a pretty little saddle horse and the first morning that I struck out for the sheep pasture for any lambs that might be due me, I had two sacks attached to the horn of my saddle. The first morning I got three lambs. I cut holes in the sacks so that their heads could protrude. I came home greatly elated at my good fortune.

Thereafter I made regular trips to the pasture before I went to school, generally getting over there about six o'clock. My fortune varied. Sometimes I would get only one and sometimes as high as four. It was some work to get them to drink, but my good mother helped me. Father, seeing our dilemma, got a lot of cow's horns. These horns were plentiful, and could be found almost anywhere in the valley.

Now, here was an ingenious piece of work. My father got these horns, washed them out and cleaned them; cut off the tips and then making a leather teat, which was attached to the tip of the horn, he put a little hole in the leather teat and attached these horns, at intervals, along the fence; then pouring milk into these horns it was no time at all until the little lambs found the milk, and after that we had no trouble feeding them. The lambs, seemingly, enjoyed their repast, for not only did they betray the utmost satisfaction in sucking the teat, but each lamb knew his own teat and they never made a mistake when going after refreshments. They always returned to the same teat at which they had previously dined. Our success and luck may be judged by the fact that in 1866 we owned eight hundred head of sheep.

When the lambs began to increase, ere we knew it we were the owners of about two hundred head and we could not spare the time to take charge of them. Accordingly, my father made arrangements with two young fellows named Hugh and Charles Daley to take over the sheep and handle them on shares. The sheep were pastured here and there and everywhere, but, at the time of my mother's death, they were pastured at Bird Creek. My father and myself went over to mark the lambs and before we finished the job we received word that mother was ill. Without finishing our task we returned home. Mother was ill but not so ill that she was confined, as yet, to her bed. However, four days after she died from pneumonia.

After procuring from Col. Hollister the discarded lambs it was not long before we had plenty of meat and of good variety. We had mutton, beef and pork.

We had a smokehouse on our place and as our killings were done principally in the fall it resulted in lots of prime smoked meats. That was the time when my mother made her soft soap sufficient to carry us over the greater part of the year.

TOWN JAIL BUILT IN JUNE 1870 AT A COST OF $190.00

CHAPTER XIII

In early days the San Juan Valley section of Monterey county
abounded with game of all kinds—My first firearms—
We fared sumptuously on poultry and fruits

AME in the San Juan Valley and surrounding districts was plentiful. There were geese, ducks, quail by the millions, cotton-tail rabbits, and the hills were full of deer. It was a hunter's paradise.

At about seven years of age I had learned to shoot—in fact, I became a very fair marksman, but my age and size precluded my carrying a heavy gun. Accordingly, I had a forked stick which I would plant on the ground and resting the gun in the fork would take aim. In due time, my father made me a gun for my own personal use. My father, who was a jack-of-all-trades, had rigged up a gunsmith shop at our place, in which he would execute many repair jobs, not only for ourselves but for the neighbors. My father got hold of a gun-barrel which he sawed off, and setting a stock to it suitable to my size, equipped me to my heart's delight. He also fixed a shot-gun for me the same way. This was when I was about eight or nine years old. In a short time I became an expert shot with a rifle and an excellent marksman with the shot-gun. Game abounded on all sides, and I kept the larder well stocked with meat of all kinds.

We carefully conserved game, in those days. There was no wanton slaughter. We only shot what we actually needed; that was sufficient.

Shortly after arriving in San Juan, and getting settled there, my mother succeeded in obtaining, from the neighbors, hen, duck, turkey and guinea hen eggs. These she set and by careful management it was not long before she had a well stocked poultry yard. She never aimed to keep more than sixty or seventy of a kind as she sold them off as quickly as the quota was reached. She had ducks, turkeys, chickens, geese and hens. So as far as the larder was concerned we feasted on domestic fowls.

Outside of pears, which we could get from the mission orchards, no fruit was obtainable except dried apples, which were dried and packed in barrels. They were a solid mass, packed in those barrels and I often wondered what would happen if someone would throw a couple of buckets of water in one of these containers.

Finding that a party had started a nursery in Santa Clara, my father went up there and succeeded in buying trees sufficient for a family orchard. He planted these trees out on two acres. The trees that my father bought were not true to name. Some were very good however, and as soon as they bore we had fruit. My mother was an expert cook, and made jams and preserves and together with wild blackberries, which were plentiful throughout that section, and which we gathered and brought home, we used to fare sumptuously in the matter of sweets.

Looking back over those years, reflection reveals the fact that even if we had plenty of fruit in those days we could not have preserved it as there were no jars or crocks or cans in which to put up the preserves.

About the year 1857-'58 there came a peddler of tinware from Watsonville, every two weeks'. The peddler's coming was a boon to us as it enabled us to secure from him the necessary receptacles wherewith to put up jellies and preserves. He would take orders for the manufacture of tinware and then bring back the order on the next trip. There was no galvanized or graniteware, everything was tin. All articles were cut and soldered, even the tea and coffee pots and milk pans.

This peddler made for my mother a colander and a two gallon can with a screw top. This can was used in my family for forty years, which speaks well for the quality of the work that the man turned out.   This can, with the screw top, was used for churning purposes—we had no churn.   We would put the milk in this can and then, after screwing the top tightly home, would agitate the can from side to side until butter formed.   It was wonderful how much butter we could obtain in this crude manner.

This tinware peddler, let it be stated here, was named Freiermuth. He was an uncle of P. J. Freiermuth and granduncle of Harry Freiermuth, who now conducts the P. J. Freiermuth hardware store in Watsonville.

THE ABBE CO. GENERAL MERCHANDISE BUILT CIRCA 1860
Photograph circa 1910

CHAPTER XIV

Early day sawmills and how they were run—First mill was a crude affair erected on Pescadero Creek—Pioneer grist mill was moved to Watsonville

N THE early part of 1850 a saw-mill was erected on Pescadero Creek—a creek that empties into the Pajaro river at the junction of Santa Clara, San Benito and Monterey counties near Chittenden. The reader must recall that, at the time I am writing about, there was no San Benito county. All that section was embraced in Monterey county, and the junction of the three counties was years afterward placed on Pescadero Creek. This saw-mill, I think, was erected by Silas Twitchell, who afterwards traded it, or sold it, to William Stingley. It was run by water-power from a large overshot wheel and had an up-and-down saw that worked in a frame, in guides. It was a very simple and crude affair. It had a contraption that moved the saw up into the log and jerked it back. There were no screws at the head-blocks; they pushed the log over by hand. There were no edgers at that time, so, in squaring the log very thick slabs would come off. The lumber wasn't cut in small dimensions; 2x4 or 4x4 were the smallest they would cut. The boards would be from twelve to thirty inches wide, and the carpenters would have to rip them to suit themselves. There was no dressing, the only dressing was by hand. It did not saw many feet in a day, and towards the fall the water would get so low that the mill had to shut down. The logs had to be brought too far and the mill was finally abandoned. Some years after being deserted a grass fire destroyed it. The land, at the present time, is owned by the William DeHart estate.

There was a great deal of split stuff hauled out of Pescadero Canyon. Nearly all the posts and pickets that were used in the San Juan Valley came out of that canyon, also the split shakes and shingles that were used.

It was up in the Pescadero Canyon that Col. W. W. Hollister and Pete Mankins had a scrap over some pickets. This occurred in the latter '50's. Mankins was a big, strong muscular man, while Hollister was tall and raw-boned. My brother saw the fight and helped to separate them. Honors were even and both fighters carried elegant black eyes for some time after.

At the mouth of this canyon, where it empties into the Pajaro river, Bill and Nels Williamson erected a grist-mill in which water-power was used, but the enterprise was a failure owing to the scarcity of water. It was afterwards torn down, moved to Watsonville and erected on the north side of the Main Street bridge at Watsonville in Santa Cruz county. This grist-mill was afterwards acquired by Robt. Orton, a miller, who subsequently became sheriff of Santa Cruz county. Bill Williamson was the grandfather of Hugh Judd, Watsonville's postmaster.

Orton sold this grist-mill to a man by the name of Thomas, who ran it for some time. I worked for him while he was conducting it.

During my stay in Watsonville I was present at the opening of the big skating rink (Folger's skating rink, afterwards the old opera house) and I was also present at the grand opening of the old Mansion House which, in those days, was one of the finest hotels in central California.

By the way, let me remark here that, during those days quite a number of relatives of mine lived on the Amesti ranch in the Pajaro Valley. There was Ike and Bob Mylar and John Hunt, all uncles of mine. Here is an interesting incident and it is a fact. My uncles were offered the Amesti ranch at $6 an acre; they refused to take it.

There was a small grist-mill built, in the early '60's, on the south side of Fourth street in San Juan, but not doing much business it soon passed out of existence.

The Bodfish canyon saw-mill, which was erected in the latter '50's, got a great deal of San Juan trade, as it had band saws and edgers.   We used to go over there and bring back much of the lumber that was used in and around San Juan. Towards the last of the '60's the Bodfish mill was conducted by Hanna & Furlong.

The mills, as run in those days, wasted much lumber. A twelve foot board, if it had a split in the end or a rotten place in it, would be thrown away, discarded, as they had nothing wherewith to cut the defective part off.   It was thrown out in the scrap pile.   Anyone could buy this kind of lumber cheaply. A two-horse load could be bought for a dollar and a four-horse load for two dollars.   Purchasers would go out to this refuse pile and pick out the best pieces.   Many a barn or out-house in the San Juan Valley was built out of this discarded material.

Another mill from which San Juan got a great deal of lumber, shingles, shakes and split stuff was a lumber mill in Brown's Valley, in the Corralitos section.   It was erected by Pruett Sinclair.   Afterwards lumber mills were erected in the Eureka Canyon section by Brown & Williamson, and another one by Rider.   White & DeHart erected a lumber mill on the White ranch, which was located on the road leading to Mount Madonna, near the Game Cock lumber mill.   There was a shingle mill near Corralitos which was run by my uncle, John Hunt.

PLAZA HALL. ZANETTA FAMILY RESIDENCE CIRCA 1874

CHAPTER XV

The doctors and lawyers in San Juan's early days were in a
class by themselves—Some, afterwards, were widely
known—Early day justices of the peace

HE DOCTORS in San Juan, in early days, as I remember them, were: Doctor F. A. McDougall, a Scotchman,, who received his education in Edinburgh, Scotland. He was a fine surgeon and physician, and was one of the old-time typical country doctors, ready to go at any time of the day or night to treat a patient. He was always at the service of anyone suffering, and it is doubtful if he ever got one-quarter of the money due him for his services. He was never known to send any patient a bill.

Dr. McDougall, whilst making a trip to Los Angeles, on one of the six-horse coaches, driven by Bob Rolls, in crossing the Gabilan range to Salinas Valley, had his shoulder dislocated. As the coach started to decend the hill the brake gave way, and Rolls, who was a first-class driver, drove the team straight down the hill instead of following the road in which case he was sure to turn over. But, at the foot of the hill there was a deep gulley and in turning to keep out of it, the stage was upset with the above result.

Dr. McDougall was brought back to San Juan, and, by his order, was strapped down and two men tried to pull his shoulder in place. They did not succeed, so he was rushed to San Francisco for treatment.

This was one case where a doctor was willing to take his own medicine.

McDougall married the widow of J. Anzar. This woman's crypt is just inside the entrance to the old mission church. She was the mother of Juan, Anatol, and P. E. G. Anzar.

P. E. G. Anzar is known at the present time throughout this section as "Lupe," and is now living at San Juan. The Anzar boys were schoolmates of mine. "Lupe" Anzar attended Santa Clara College in 1868, and left it in 1870. At that time he established, with Pablo Vacca, a wholesale butcher business in Los Angeles. He also ran a livery stable in that city before returning to San Juan in 1876. He married Mrs. Wm. Breen, who was the daughter of Angelo Zanetta, and was the widow of William Breen, the youngest son of Patrick Breen.

Mr. Anzar's marriage occurred in January, 1877. This date I remember distinctly as I had married about a month earlier. About a year ago the Anzars celebrated their golden wedding anniversary, and an immense crowd attended the celebration.

Another doctor was a man by the name of Hart, an Englishman. He, also, was educated in Edinburgh, Scotland, about the same time as Dr. McDougall. If I remember aright they were schoolmates. He was a fine physician, but very eccentric. He lived with our family for quite awhile. He had a diploma, printed on genuine sheepskin and written in latin. It was in a tin case and having been immersed in sea water, by the accidental sinking of a boat, I think at Australia, the sheepskin had become wrinkled. I remember now, with some amusement, an incident concerning this diploma. Dr. Hart, not liking its wrinkled appearance, asked my mother for a hot flatiron, and attempted to smooth it out. The result was disastrous, as when it was smoothed out it became so hard and thick that it would no longer fit in the tin receptacle.

Dr. Hart slept in a room adjoining the room I occupied, and as the partition between the two rooms was thin, I could hear everything going on in his room. Every night he would repeat a fervent and eloquent prayer before retiring and then, after getting up off his knees, would curse with all the vehemence of an outraged man's nature, Mary Jane Shelland. Evidently she was some fair damsel who had figured in an episode in the early life of the doctor. He never discussed the matter, so I never learned the true inwardness of this outbreak of profanity.

He was a clever doctor, but his practice suffered greatly from the fact that people were afraid of him, as often he would be found walking along the road and cursing Mary Jane Shelland. He was a great walker. He would think nothing of walking from San Juan to San Francisco, where he went on periodical sprees. From these trips he would return in a somewhat dilapidated condition and relate, with great gusto, the encounter he had had with some police officer in which, of course, he came off second best, and got locked up in the calaboose.

Joe C. Gilman, now a resident of Watsonville, who in the early days, drove the stage between Watsonville and Gilroy over what was then known as the old San Jose route, which ran over the mountains via Mount Madonna relates that on one of his trips, he met Dr. Hart, who was stepping out in lively fashion, for San Francisco. Joe, knowing Dr. Hart, pulled up his team and queried, "Don't you want a ride?"

Hart looked at him and said: "No. I'm in a hurry and want to get to San Francisco quick!"

It took Joe sometime to recover from that sally, as he considered himself a right smart, pert, fast-driving jehu.

Another doctor in the San Juan Valley was the late Doctor Thos. Flint, but he seldom practiced medicine. The only time that I ever remember Doctor Flint to respond to a call was on one occasion when a driver for Col. Hollister met with an accident in "The Lane." He was attempting to fix some furniture that had gotten loose on his wagon-load, and in so doing one of the pieces tumbled down and struck a horse. The startled team ran away. In the runaway the man was run over, one of the wheels passing over his chest. Doctor Flint responded to this call and treated the man. *

A little later came Doctor Simmons. He had a son and daughter who attended school with me. The son's name was Elmer and the daughter's name was Clara. Doctor Simmons afterwards moved to Watsonville where Clara married John Brown, and the son, after graduating from the Pajaronian office, as a printer, went to San Francisco, and in time became the head man (manager) of the great oil and paint firm of the Whittier, Fuller Co. He has since retired from active business pursuits. Dr. Simmons was not only a first-class doctor but a pharmacist of no mean ability. He opened a drug store in Watsonville and conducted it there for years.

During the never-to-be-forgotten smallpox epidemic of 1868, which assumed a deadly form in this section, extending from Santa Cruz to Watsonville, San Jose and other places, there was in San Juan a doctor Westfall. He afterwards moved to Monterey. I believe this doctor is dead now.

There was another physician there, a Dr. Johnson, of Gilroy, and then came Dr. C. G. Cargill. Between Doctor Johnson's time and the advent of Doctor Cargill a number of other physicians had located in San Juan whose names and careers I have forgotten. They would come and go, and it was very hard to keep track of them.

The lawyers that figured in San Juan's early history were W. E. Lovett, a brother-in-law of Llewellyn Bixby. While he

---

* (The Pajaronian editor was proud, during his sojourn in Hollister, to call Doctor Flint his friend. The doctor often stepped into the "Free Lance" office when we were conducting that paper, and occasionally related to us some of his experiences as a physician. He was one of the most unassuming and entertaining men we have ever met.)

had but little law practice in San Juan, he figured prominently in the star route scandals that were being investigated in Washington, D. C., in the middle '60's.

Another lawyer there was a Mr. Blair, who had but little practice, and finally went away.

George W. Crane was another practicing attorney. Crane was a highly educated man, and a southerner from Virginia. He had been a partner with Attorney Peckham in Santa Cruz. Peckham afterwards moved to San Jose.

Judge Crane—he was always styled "Judge"—married the widow of Dr. Sanford. Previous to her marriage to Sanford she was the wife of Sanchez, one of the most noted characters in the San Juan Valley, in the early days. The Sanchez family was a large one, many of its descendants are living today in Hollister and other places in San Benito county. When the widow Sanchez married Judge Crane she was already the mother of five children. Four of the children were by Sanchez. She bore one child to Dr. Sanford.

One of the Sanchez girls married Dan Wilson, another married T. J. McKnight and the third married Jas. H. Roache. This last girl was a twin sister of Gregorio Sanchez.

Gregorio Sanchez married Margaret Breen, daughter of Samuel Breen. The fifth child, whose name was Fidella Sanford, married Jas. Breen, a brother of Mrs. Greg Sanchez.

Whenever any case of importance transpired, outside legal talent was imported. I remember amongst the imported legal talent Woodside and Gregory; also a lawyer by the name of Webb, these resided at Monterey; sometimes Julius Lee, from Watsonville, would come over.

Constables were so numerous, that is, they changed so often, that I failed to keep track of them. It must be remembered that in those days there were no salaries attached to the office, the only remuneration being the fees they received from serving papers which fees were anything but munificent. No one wanted the constable's job unless they had another job on the side, for in addition to its being illy-paid, there was, to a certain extent, considerable danger attached to the office. A constable never knew when he would be called upon to face a "bad man" and arrest him.

Regarding the Justices of the Peace, I remember the following: George Chalmers, John Birmingham, John Whitney (who was also postmaster for many years), and Joe Heritage.

John Gaster, one of the first justices of the peace, of San Juan, died in San Juan in 1868, during the smallpox epidemic.

The first constable I remember was James Miller and the last one, the present incumbent "CC" Zanetta.

The supervisors received $5.00 per day, when in session, and a mileage of 15c a mile one way. Their sessions generally occupied about three days every month. There was no money in this job, either, for the supervisors had to pay their way to Monterey, at that time the county seat, and also their board and lodging whilst engaged in their work as supervisors. It must be remembered that in those days all that region was embraced in Monterey County. Accordingly, in view of the poor pay attached to official jobs it may well be judged that there was very little money paid out to secure elections. Votes were not bought in those days.

CHAPTER XVI

*The pony express riders of early days—Civil war clouds gather-
ing—San Juan was dubbed a "Copperhead" town
Troops sent to mission town to quell trouble*

N 1860 the mail came from San Francisco. It took
26 days for mail from New York City, through the
isthmus, to reach San Francisco. Then the Pony
Express was started—I think in April, 1860. It
started from San Francisco at this end and St. Joseph, Missouri,
on the other side. The trip was made across the continent in
ten days. That time was afterwards considerably shortened but
I remember how highly elated the people were at the prospect
of getting their mail in ten days instead of waiting for the
twenty-six days.

The Pony Express riders rode day and night, changing riders and horses at certain stations. We would often hear of these
brave, fearless, men being massacred by Indians.

In 1861, a memorable year and one that I will always
remember, dissension over the slavery question broke out between
the Northern and Southern states. A joint resolution had been
passed by the State Legislature, in response from a request from
the President, to put down the foes of the central government.
So in all towns and cities military organizations were raised.
San Juan, however, did not organize any military company.
It was often dubbed a "Copperhead Town." The people who
had settled in San Juan were mostly southerners and western
people, and their sympathies were with the South.

These southern sympathizers were men and women who,
facing great hardships, had crossed the continent to leave as an
heritage to their children the grand and glorious state of California—the most wonderful state in the Union.

The Democrats were in the majority in San Juan.   At all times both parties, Republican and Democrats, in that section had lived together peaceably and amicably.   They were neighbors, friends, and in many cases, partners in business. So, accordingly, everything ran along peaceably and smoothly in the San Juan Valley until 1864 when the government hired the National Hotel (at that time vacant) to be used as a barracks.   It was called Camp Lowe, after Frederick Lowe who was governor of this state at that time.   Three companies, two of infantry and one of cavalry under the command of Major J. C. Cremony, came to San Juan and the town took on a military aspect.

You can imagine how excited we boys were at this invasion, and the interest we took in seeing the soldiers parade and go through their maneuvers.   The principal reason for sending the troops to San Juan was to look into the activities of two men who claimed to be confederate soldiers, but who, in reality, were nothing else but "freebooters" of the meanest type.

These two men roamed around San Juan, Panoche, San Benito, Paicines, Tres Pinos, and the New Idria Mines.   They boasted of murders they had committed, but their chief pastime was to slit the ears of anyone whom they disliked.   They continued to rob and plunder and the civil authorities could do nothing with them.   Finally, complaint reaching the Federal authorities, troops were sent to San Juan to take charge of the situation.

The advent of these soldiers was "duck soup" to the San Juanites.   Old man Kemp kept a saloon on the opposite corner from the National Hotel and ran a big, steep poker game.   The soldiers seeking amusement would engage in poker at Kemp's saloon, and the $13.00 a month that the Government was paying them soon disappeared.   The officers had their own poker games and they were also stripped of their salaries by the male members of San Juan's elite society.   Consequently, the invasion by the troops was not as bad as was at first anticipated.

The entire contingent were royal good fellows, although the town calaboose was constantly crowded with drunken soldiers. The officers were gentlemen and everyone liked them.

While the troops were there I remember that three of San Juan's citizens made some remarks that were considered somewhat treasonable. These three men were promptly arrested and imprisoned in a guard-house (an old adobe that had been obtained for such a purpose). However, the incarceration of these men did not last long for the guards placed over them fell asleep and the prisoners escaped. It was significant that the guards made no report of the escape until the men had had ample time to get "o'er the hills, and far away." And they were never caught. We were always of the opinion that filthy lucre had crossed the palms of those guards.

The officers made a big splurge about recapturing these fugitives and orders were issued to search every home in San Juan, but after the soldiers searched two or three houses they quit.

It was while searching for these three men that had escaped that a squad of the soldiers, away up in the mountains, under the command of Lieut. Rafferty, came upon the two rascals whose depredations had originally brought the troops to San Juan. After a running fight of several miles the two fugitives escaped in the wilderness.

Major Cremony left soon after the above events transpired and went to Arizona to fight the Apaches. The alleged confederate soldiers and robbers were subsequently captured by Capt. McIlroy and a squad of United States soldiers at Los Angeles. Capt. McIlroy was, in after years, the owner of the hotel at Emmett, on the road to the New Idria Mines which place he sold to Tom Ingels, brother of the late Mrs. M. B. Tuttle of Watsonville.

Eventually the soldiers went away, and peace once more reigned over the San Juan Valley.

Sometime in the '60's a large number of settlers came into the San Juan Valley and settled at its lower end. By the lower end I mean that part of the valley extending from the old mission towards Chittenden Pass. Amongst these new settlers whom I remember were James T. Collins, W. Prescott, father of ex-Supervisor W. S. Prescott; John Salthouse who was the uncle of the treasurer of San Benito County, the late Jack Welch, (Salthouse left Welch 80 acres in the San Juan Valley adjoining the Prescott property) "Josh" Bean; the Lynch family, whose children, Bill, Susie, and Nancy, attended the same school I did; Frank and John Jordan, whose two children, Amanda and John, also went to school with me; Frank Ross, afterwards sheriff of San Benito County; the Craw and Moore families; the Canfield family; Dr. Matthews; John Rupe, who settled there in Monterey County in 1853, in what was afterwards known as the San Felipe section. He came over into the San Juan Valley and married Dr. Matthew's daughter. Dr. Matthew lived a short distance west of the present Dowdy farm on the San Juan and Sargent road.

In this lower part of the San Juan Valley which was too far for the children to go to school in San Juan, the settlers organized a district and built their own school. A Miss Burns, who taught the school, boarded with the Odom family who lived in this district close to the school. At twelve o'clock one night Jim Collins, returning from a lodge meeting perceived this dwelling on fire. It was entirely destroyed and all the members of the family, including the teacher, were burned to death. The unfortunate victims, Mrs. Odom, her three children and Miss Burns, the teacher, were all buried in the same grave. Mr. Odom was away from home, at the time, on business. The origin of the fire was always a mystery. Some theorized that they were murdered, and the house set on fire; others that the tragedy was the result of an accident. Miss Burns was a great reader and often read far into the night. It was thought that possibly she fell asleep and the candle by which she was reading turned over and set fire to the house.

CHAPTER XVII

Road to Salinas Valley—Manuel Larios' fiesta days—Indian
women did the washing in primitive style—
The late John Breen

THE PRESENT San Juan cemeteries are located on the old "El Camino Real". This road in the early days was the overland route to the southern portion of the state. The stages, or conveyances, after passing the cemeteries turned into the canyon and ascended the steep grade up the Gabilan mountains—so steep that invariably, if the stage was crowded, the men had to walk up the hill. Women were treated chivalrously in those days and were not requested to leave the stage at all. At the foot of the descent, on the other side of the Gabilan range, the road traversed a canyon, emerging at what was known as Hebbron's Lake, passed through Natividad, and struck out for Soledad and San Luis Obispo.

On this road there were several old settlers whom I shall mention:

On the left of the road after passing the cemetery, situated on a plateau, was the home of Manuel Larios. It was a two-story adobe house with a large room for dancing purposes on the lower floor. It would be well to remark, right here, that all the adobe haciendas of the early days had similar dancing rooms on the lower floor, in fact, in those days, these haciendas were places at which friends and neighbors often gathered to have a good time. Don Larios always gave a fiesta on the 16th of September, which was the day of Mexican independence. He would announce a bull fight but the bull fight did not amount to much. The fiesta was the thing.

The Spaniards (we called them "Spaniards") were common figures in the early days. They were constantly coming and going and made up a large portion of the population. They all had good horses and at their fiestas I have seen them do all kinds of stunts.

At this fiesta a big fire would be started, a beef killed and barbecued, and the meat hung up in some convenient place. All hands would repair to the meat, cutting off as much as they wanted to eat, and, with bread, have a meal at their pleasure. It is worthy of remark that at these festive gatherings it was rarely that any of the guests would be seen drunk.

The music, comprising violins and guitars, was placed in a big room in the house and one could dance until he was exhausted. Everything connected with the fiesta was free, and all, whether invited or not, were made welcome—that is, if they behaved themselves.

Larios was one of the old Dons. He was a fine Castilian gentleman, a man of many virtues, respected and beloved by all who knew him.

Continuing on this road a little further past Larios' place was a residence occupied by a man named Benjamin Holliwell. In 1868 this residence was empty having been deserted by its owner and during the great smallpox epidemic was used as a pesthouse until, subsequently, another pesthouse was built on the bank of the San Benito river near the site where Ben Flint, Jr., afterwards built his home.

At the foot of the hill on this road there was located another home occupied by a family by the name of Stramner, who were early settlers in that section. The two daughters, named respectively Sinai and Lucy, attended school with me, in San Juan.

It will be remembered that there were three grades going over the mountain;[16]the old grade that I have just spoken about; then, afterwards, there was another grade that went over

Raggio's Canyon and the third grade that was taken over by the state and made the present grade.

At the foot of the second grade you came first to the home of Bob Mylar, my uncle. Afterwards this home was occupied by James Smith who later was elected sheriff of Monterey County; Smith, subsequently, moved away.

After Smith's removal old man Raggio took over the place.

A short distance west of the Raggio place was the home of a man by the name of Daley. Daley had four sons whose names were Hugh, Charlie, Henry and James. They all attended school during my school days. The Daley family were the poorest folks I ever knew. Yet, strange to relate, these four boys, equipped poorly by education to encounter the vicissitudes of life, took sheep on shares and eventually became very wealthy. They moved over into the San Joaquin Valley, living in the vicinity of Hanford.

Returning to my father's place, on the other side of San Juan, at the junction of the road where it turned and ran on to Hollister, in one direction, and up to the Flint ranch, or, as it was called, the Flint Home in the other direction, there was located, in early days, a number of Indian huts. From this settlement the place was always designated as "Indian Corners."

The women did laundry work. They washed clothes on a smooth board two feet wide and three feet long with one end of the board in the creek that ran down past my father's place from the San Juan Canyon, and the other end of the board was slightly raised. They would get down on their knees and rub and scrape these clothes until they were clean, using nothing but cold water. At first they used the "amole" or "soap root" which they dug out of the ground up in the hills, but as this began to be scarce they used soap. After getting the clothes clean they would spread them on the grass to dry. I never saw cleaner or whiter clothes than garments washed by these Indian women. On Saturday afternoons they would be seen going into San Juan with big bundles of clean clothes balanced on top of their heads, which they were delivering to their patrons in the village. The Indian men did odd jobs.

There was another location in the lower end of the valley, which also contained a number of these Indian families. With this latter aggregation there lived an old Indian who claimed to be over one hundred years of age, and who made a pilgrimage to San Juan every day riding a jackass. Suspended from the saddle were two rawhide bags, each of which held about one-half bushel. He would ride along slowly stopping at every house that he came to, and it became a custom for the residents, when they saw the old fellow stop in front of their homes, to come out and give him something, bread, meat, or whatever they could afford. The consequence was that although the old Indian never solicited charity, and rarely uttered a word, he would return home in the evening loaded down with provender. This old man was a striking figure. His age made his skin look like yellow parchment and he had no teeth. His venerable appearance always inspired respect. He claimed to be one of the Indians who had worked on the old Mission when it was being constructed.

Some of these men were large, strong, and of fine physique. They were excellent workers in the harvest. I only remember them as Indians, (although I knew them well personally) by the names of "Frank, ' "Pete," "John,"' etc.

However, I remember that one of them was shot dead on Third Street, in San Juan, by Ambrosio Rosas, who defended his action by declaring that he was in fear of losing his life at the hands of the Indian. Rosas was acquitted.

Another Indian I remember was killed by Benino Soto, who also claimed self-defense and was likewise acquitted.

Another one of those Indians, a big fellow whom I knew by the name of Frank, disputed the right-of-way with a South-

ern Pacific train near Pescadero creek; and was killed. The
verdict was exactly the same as the two foregoing cases. The
engine was acquitted.

These Indians are today about extinct. Is it not strange
that where these simple people come into contact with our so-
called civilization they gradually disappear?

To the east of town and just outside the town's limits,
stood, and is still standing, the residence of John Breen. The
house stands back from the road leading from San Juan to
Hollister, about a quarter of a mile. John Breen was born in
Canada. In 1852 he married Miss Leigh Margaret Smith.
Mr. Breen was the son of Patrick Breen, the head of the Breens,
of the Donner party. John Breen was a supervisor of Monterey County, and after San Benito County was created was supervisor from the San Juan precinct for years, occupying, from
time to time, the position of chairman of the board.

A more honest and incorruptible man than John Breen
never lived in San Benito County. He was a very unassuming
man, spoke but little, and when he did speak he talked directly
to the point. He did not decide without due deliberation and
once his mind was made up nothing could move him. San
Benito County owes much to John Breen, for due to his careful manipulation of its finances, coupled with a desire to advance its progress, it owes much of its present prosperity.

John Breen's farm and my father's farm joined, and a
finer neighbor we never knew. When the proposition to run
the road from San Juan to the lane was broached, Breen, who
had had dealings with my father before, and found them very
satisfactory, came forward and told my father that he would
give, free, all the property necessary for the road, and for my
father not to bother with it at all. This action demonstrated
the friendship of the man and his kindly consideration of other
people. The giving of the land would have materially cut
down my father's place but Breen insisted on giving the land
from his place.

Many of those reading my memoirs will remember the place called "Breen's Grove." It used to be the custom to hold the Fourth of July celebrations first in San Juan, and then in Hollister. At San Juan these celebrations were always held in "Breen's Grove." This land was originally my father's but by an amicable arrangement Breen bought the twenty acres from him upon which the grove was located.

I may say here in passing that many good times were had in that old grove, for a picnic at San Juan attracted the countryside, and everyone who attended a picnic at that grove had lots of fun.

Do any of my readers remember the Jim Roache place? It was situated on the road that connected with the Lane leading to Hollister. [17] It was a double house, two stories high, and was built by Marselle and John Bixby. This place was located on what was supposed to be government land. It was land that Colonel Hollister advised my father to take up. Whether the Bixbys preempted the land I cannot say. It was afterwards taken over in the San Justo grant. I stayed there many nights as the Bixby men were away a great portion of the time with their sheep and John's wife was frightened at staying alone. The Bixbys did not live in this house very long. They afterwards went to southern California where, by lucky investments, in real estate they became immensely wealthy.

CHAPTER XVIII.

*San Juan from 1860 to 1870—The starting of the Overland
Stage Line from San Francisco to Los Angeles—
A perilous trip in bad weather*

HAVE already related, as far back as I can remember, certain incidents in connection with my stay in San Juan from 1855-60. I have carefully gone over the streets and endeavored to convey a picture of San Juan as it existed in those days, noting the various buildings, streets, and the people who resided there.

I now take up San Juan from 1860 to 1870.

In the early 60's there passed through San Juan, coming and going, hosts of would-be settlers. Some were from the mines in the north, others from southern California. These people were looking for places whereon to settle. Some had already settled in other parts of the state, but becoming dissatisfied with their location had abandoned their claims or sold them and started out to find a more acceptable home-site. In addition to these people there were many strangers crossing the plains and coming into California.

As San Juan was one of the most important stopping places on El Camino Real, it steadily grew larger and larger.

It was in the year 1861, if I remember aright, that Flint, Bixby & Co., established their line of Overland Stages,[18]running from San Francisco to Los Angeles. This line was under the superintendency of William Buckley, who managed the same for many years.

The advent of the Overland Stages added a new impetus to San Juan. The Overland Company needed horses, and feed, and gave employment to hundreds of men, adding greatly to the town's revenue. Accordingly, San Juan being one of the stopping places on the route, it went ahead at an amazing rate.

San Juan was made the stage company's headquarters, as it was the first stopping place of the stage. The stage arrived there today and would start on its return to San Francisco tomorrow morning.

The stages would arrive about five-thirty in the afternoon, and the passengers would dine in San Juan, whilst their baggage was being transferred to another six-horse coach, which, after the meal, would start south.

I have often, when a boy, saw those stages start south, in the winter time, when it was dark and stormy. The stage was only dimly lighted having but two lights—a lamp on either side of the driver's seat. Underneath the driver's seat was carried the express box and the U. S. mail, this was covered with a leather apron which the driver would pull up in wet weather to his chin, as would any other passenger that was occupying the seat beside him. This would shed off the rain along the somewhat perilous trip. There was nothing else to protect the driver from the wind and rain save a rubber coat, but he started out bravely for an all-night's drive.

There were no springs underneath the bodies of the coaches, they were thoroughbrace, that is, the body of the coach rested on several thicknesses of leather which served to ward off, from the passengers, many a jolt. But, Lord, how those coaches would rock to and fro as they bowled along the primitive roads; and yet, they were easy to ride in!

The "boot" in the rear of the coach which held the trunks, valises, etc., was covered by a heavy leather apron which was strapped solidly over them.

Two of these coaches, "The Great Eastern," and "The Great Western," would carry sixteen passengers, four to a seat, inside; two passengers could ride, with the driver, and three on a seat on top of the stage, behind the driver, and three on a seat over the baggage "boot" behind, but these three had to ride backwards. There was a little iron rail that ran around the top of the coach, and many a time when there were more passengers that the coach could carry inside, passengers would sit on the top of the coach and allow their legs to dangle over the side.

I once made a trip on one of these stages from San Jose to San Juan when there were twenty-nine passengers aboard the stage.

The company generally had two or three drivers stopping at the Plaza Hotel, and when the occasion arose they would relieve a congested stage by putting a small one out in charge of one of these drivers. It can be imagined that at this time, the Plaza Hotel was doing a thriving business. The barroom was crowded night and day. Some of the passengers would lay over there to rest, and to take in all the points of interest in that vicinity.

In those days, travelers—men and women alike—wore long linen dusters, tightly buttoned up, even closely drawn around the neck in order to keep off the dust which at times was almost smothering.

When the passengers on the Overland Stages arrived at the Plaza Hotel they generally rushed to the wash room, although, in many instances, the male passengers would stop long enough at the bar to first wash out their throats.

About this time Frank Fulgium bought the National Hotel from Gaster, the man who originally erected the structure, and opened it up as a hostelry. Fulgium was also interested in a freight business that conveyed merchandise between Alviso and the New Idria Mines. It will be remembered that Harris, who conducted a merchandise store had a contract for furnishing purchases and goods to the mines.

E. A. Reynolds a leading sheep and stockman in San Juan, about this time, bought the block bounded by Second and Third, Tuolumne and Jefferson Streets, formerly owned by Clark.

Geo. Russell, his son-in-law, built a residence on Second Street on the property. E. A. Reynolds was, at one time, a supervisor of Monterey county from the San Juan district.

Property on all sides was changing hands and San Juan was commencing to boom.

All the stages owned by the company were driven out of San Juan with matched teams. Superintendent Buckley was a great stickler for uniformity and these four or six-horse teams were always either white, sorrel, bay, or roan teams.

Each driver furnished and owned his own whip. These whips served as marks of distinction. They were of the finest quality, silver-tipped, and the majority of them had a silver band for each year that its owner had been a driver. Some of these drivers graduated from the old Overland Stage Company, and they were veritable sons of Jehu, mentioned in biblical lore.

The Stage Company had its own horse-shoer with headquarters at San Juan. This horse-shoer, Jimmy McInerny, was one of the best horse-shoers that I have ever seen. It was his duty to go along the stage line as far south as San Luis Obispo and look after the shoes on the horses at the various stations after which he would return to San Juan. How true this is I don't know, but it was one of the legends of San Juan that Jimmy McInerny was known to have shod sixteen horses in a day—and if that is true, Jimmy did a day's work!

CHAPTER XIX

*The hotels of San Juan in its early days—The opening date
of the Plaza Hotel was a big event—Sports on the Plaza
—Spanish costumes in early days.*

N JUNE 24, 1856, the Plaza Hotel was opened by Angelo Zanetta, whom we have referred to, elsewhere, as having run the Sebastopol Hotel, on Third Street.

The Plaza Hotel was originally the home of the Anzar family, and in it P. E. G. Anzar was born. Upon the death of his parents the property was left to him. Zanetta purchased the property from Anzar's guardian—he being under age, at the time. When Zanetta purchased this building it was occupied by a merchandise firm conducted by Jas. McMahon and a man named Griffin.

After tearing off the top and remodeling the first story, the second story was added to it, this story being built of lumber. There was a veranda the entire length of the building, in front. This veranda, on festival days, was always occupied by interested spectators of the bull and bear fights and other games. Generally these fights occurred on June 24th, of each year, that date being St. John's Day.

The opening of the Plaza Hotel was a gala affair, the place was crowded, as Angelo Zanetta was well and favorably known not only in Monterey, from which place he had come to San Juan, but also in the San Juan Valley.

From the ranchos, far and near, came the Dons with their families. To me, a boy of eight years, it was a great sight. A band was engaged and played on the veranda of the hotel for the delectation of the populace. The veranda was crowded with senoritas and women of other nationalities, all in gay attire.

After attending mass in the morning at the old mission, which fronts on the plaza, the fun would commence.

The gay cabelleros, gaudily attired and riding finely comparisoned horses, would display their horsemanship in many ways. Backing up some distance they would ride on the plaza at full speed and pick up money, handkerchiefs, and even, as related before, pluck a chicken's head from its body— the chicken being buried in the ground with only its head above the surface.

PLAZA HOTEL WITH WELLS FARGO IN THE 1860'S

In order to make the celebration as noisy and as impressive as possible the old cannon, to which I have alluded before, was raised from the ground and placed on the back part of a wagon, the two wheels of which had been fixed up for the occasion. The idea in doing this was to load it with more ease. This cannon was fired at regular intervals all day and away into the night, and of course this bombardment was a great attraction for us youngsters.

Here and there could be seen, on these occasions, a Don attired in a serape (a serape was a finely made blanket with a hole in the center through which the head of the wearer was thrust). Some of these cloaks (serapes) were very valuable. They were made of the finest materials, and had silk worked into them as well as being ornamented in various ways. They were rated highly and commanded a big price.

The Mexicans were given to wearing broad-brimmed hats, most of which came from Chile and Mexico.

The bulls were kept in a pen connected with the main corral, and the bear that was to mix things with the bull, was generally kept away some distance from the plaza in a building selected for that purpose. The bear was in a cage which was kept on the carreta, and when the time arrived for the combat to begin the carreta was drawn into the corral, the bear safely tied to a stake in the ground, and the cage and carreta taken away.

One of the great fiestas in the old town was St. John's day, June 24th, each year. St. John was the patron saint of the village. For this event great preparations were made and a big celebration arranged for. It was the annual event to which every youngster in the village looked forward to. The third and last day was always marked by the bull-fighting. The climax of the program was a grand bull-and-bear fight. In those days the Vaqueros would arrange to go over to the Quien Sabe Rancho, now owned by the D. E. Laveaga family (who by the way, it is said, got that wonderfully rich domain in exchange for a billiard table), and there the Vaqueros would capture a grizzly bear for the celebration. The grizzlies in those days used to come down onto the plains to feed, and the San Juan boys would take over a carreta, the clumsily constructed, two-wheeled vehicles used in those days. They would lasso the bear and securely tie him and would bring him back in the carreta to San Juan, where he would be confined until wanted on the day of the celebration. A large enclosure would be constructed on the plaza inside of which bull fighting would be indulged in. The bull fights in those days were not marked by the brutality seen at the bull fights in Spain. The mission padres would not permit any brutality. The sport was largely in the shape of feats of horsemanship pitted against the onrushes of the bull and the agility of the matadores to get out of the way of the enraged animal's onslaught.

On the day of the bear fight the bear would be attached to a pole in the center of the enclosure. He would have a run of about twenty feet around the pole to which he was attached by a strong riata. The bull was similarly tethered by one foot. Invariably, the bear would be killed inasmuch as he would stand on his hind feet to receive the oncoming bull who would, with so fair a target before him, generally rip the bear open after a few thrusts. The bull usually escaped with a few scratches, although I have seen some of the bulls so badly mangled that they had to be killed. I have seen as many as 5000 people attend one of these fiestas. They came from all directions, far and near. Where they slept or how they got food to eat, I do not know and I often wondered if Providence sent ravens to feed them.

When a boy I was sitting on a fence watching the proceedings at one of these festivals, and witnessed a premature explosion of the cannon which tore off Lon Woodworth's arm, below the elbow. Lon Woodworth was a son-in-law of Joshua Twitchell.

In order to load the cannon, which was greatly heated, from being fired so often, a man would place his thumb over the vent to keep it from prematurely exploding. At the time of this accident a man by the name of Hopper was engaged in stopping up the vent. Hooper had evidently been "indulging" rather freely and as Woodworth rammed home the charge the cannon exploded, with the result above stated.

After the grand celebration of the opening of the Plaza Hotel, on June 24, 1856 we had a hotel that we considered second to none. Zanetta became noted throughout the entire state for his cuisine. The Plaza Hotel became the headquarters for traders in sheep, horses, cattle and hogs. They were a free spending lot, those men, and San Juan did well by their trade.

The purchases made by these buyers were for the San Francisco and San Jose markets. The cattle were driven overland to their ultimate destination.

The fame of the hotel, under Zanetta, spread. It was noteworthy that drummers would come to San Juan, make their reservations there, and then hiring a horse and buggy would interview their customers in Santa Cruz, Watsonville, Salinas and other points, always managing to return to San Juan by night fall. Some of these drummers would make the Plaza Hotel their headquarters for several days. This was due, mainly to the fine table set by Zanetta, the excellent wines and liquors that he kept, and the air of hospitality that pervaded the entire establishment.

Years afterwards a laughable incident occurred at the Plaza Hotel. The entrance, into the hotel, one afternoon, of a scared steer that not only drove all the lounging inmates out but when roped to be led out the side door, was found standing up at the bar. This gave rise to the story that the steer, which had broken away from a herd that was being driven through the plaza, had came in for a drink and Tony Taix, who was running the hotel at that time, treated the animal so royally that he was decidedly groggy when finally led away.

Soon after the hotel was opened by Zanetta, John Comfort bought a half interest in it with him.

Shortly after going into partnership Zanetta and Comfort built, facing the plaza opposite the Plaza Hotel, a two-story frame building the upper story of which was used as a dance hall. For years following, the Plaza dance hall of San Juan was rated as having the finest dancing floor in that section of California.

Adjoining this dance hall was a large stable that had been used by the Overland Stage Company. This stable was acquired by Zanetta and Comfort. Prior to this Zanetta and Comfort had conducted a stable back of the hotel. This stable fronted on Third Street and was directly opposite the old Sebastopol Hotel.

East of the Plaza Hotel in the same block, was the long two-story adobe that formerly was the home and headquarters of General Castro, and afterwards the home of the Breen family. This building also had a veranda that faced on the plaza. The Breen family, that came across the plains in the Donner party, occupied this large building. The only Breen that was not a member of the Donner party was Wm. Breen. He was born in San Juan.

After the death of Patrick Breen and his wife, the children one by one went away and finally the old building was deserted. This building is still owned by the Breen family.

After the Breen family went away the building was placed in charge of Mrs. O'Flynn, one of the finest Irish women that I ever knew. It was during Mrs. O'Flynn's incumbency of the Breen home as caretaker that Helen Hunt Jackson, authoress of "Ramona," came to San Juan and laid the foundation of that famous novel around San Juan. After Ramona's authoress left San Juan I learned, with great regret, that she had made some unkind remarks about Mrs. O'Flynn. This I resented deeply for I had known Mrs. O'Flynn from the time she had arrived in San Juan, a widow with four small children. She was a good Catholic, a fine woman of irreproachable character, and she worked her hands to the bone for her children, whom she raised in splendid style. They were always neatly dressed and clean and she gave them the best education she could afford. They grew up fine members of society and moved away. I lost track of them after their removal.

I have never had, since that time, any use whatsoever for the authoress of "Ramona." I always thought that Mrs. O'Flynn was a woman deserving of the highest commendation. She supported her children and brought them up by her hard work at the wash tub. She took in washing early and late, day after day, following that occupation with only one object in view—the health and happiness of her children.

CHAPTER XX

Various phases of life in San Juan during 1861-1862—The wet winter of 1862—The disastrous drought of 1864—My first railroad ride.

T THIS time San Juan boasted of two blacksmith shops running full blast. One was conducted by Jasper Twitchell, the other by W. G. Hubbard. Many new saloons had been opened and some of them were kept open all night. Gambling flourished and San Juan boomed as one of the most enterprising towns on the route of the Overland Stage Company.

The stores of that period (1855-1860) carried general assortments—there were no ready-to-wear women's garments. They bought the materials and made up the garments at home, by hand, at first, until the advent of the sewing machine, which was some years later. It was not uncommon to see a woman or her daughter continuously sewing, on garments, even at night, in the home circle. Of course, if it was a very fine dress that was to be made, it was taken to the dressmaker.

The Spanish women excelled in needlework and their drawn-work was incomparable. If you got a peep at their undergarments, they were immaculate and starched until they rattled. There were no coats worn by the ladies, they all wore shawls of different grades. Some were woolen, while others were of the finest silk. Men's suits could be bought in the store. Men's work shirts were piled on the counter; if you wanted to buy one you picked it up and held it in front of you with a cuff in each hand and arms extended. It the tail was long enough and the sleeves about right, you bought it regardless of size of the collar. Shirts were, generally, all the same color; either small check or hickory. Ties were seldom worn.

White shirts for dress purposes had the collar attached which was worn as a standing collar. Boots were worn by all men. They were on display in boxes on the floor along the counter and were bought something like the shirts. You found the style you wanted and tried on pair after pair until you got a fit. You did not pay any attention to sizes and if the merchant had anything to attend to, he let you alone until you found a pair that would satisfy you. It was told on one of the prominent merchants in town, at that time, that someone bought a pair of boots on credit and the merchant forgot who it was, so he charged them up to all his credit customers. If any of them made a kick about it he would scratch the item off their bill. I often wondered how many times he got paid for those boots.

Very little tobacco could be bought except plug tobacco. You would scarcely find an American who used cigarettes. Most of them chewed, however, and if they smoked a pipe they cut their tobacco off a plug. There was no order about the stores in early days. They would have what you wanted somewhere, and it was up to you to find it.

About this same period or a little later, William Palmtag, the Hollister banker who died recently, was running a brewery wagon, for his uncle, Chris Palmtag, between Watsonville and San Juan. "Billy" would make one or two trips every week. His uncle conducted the brewery at the foot of Main Street, adjacent to the Bridge across the Pajaro river in Watsonville. The beer in those days was delivered in five and ten-gallon kegs. Such a thing as bottled beer was unknown.

About the same time Stephen Martinelli, of Watsonville, also made one or two trips each week to San Juan to sell his famous cider champagne, bottled pop, and sarsaparilla. In those days "soda-pop" was confined in a bottle with a string tied over the cork and when the string was cut the cork shot out of the bottle with a report akin to a pistol shot. However, soft drinks were used but very little in those days. They were a hardy lot, those pioneers and they took their's straight. The liquor, as a general thing, was pure; and oh, Lordy! how some of those early Argonauts could get away with it.   Still they seldom got drunk!

The winter of 1861-1862 was the wettest winter that I ever witnessed in California.   It rained incessantly for days. Everything was tied up.   Teamsters plying between Alviso and San Juan had their teams stuck in the mud.   They would bring their horses into town and had to stop there until weather conditions permitted them to move their loaded wagons.[19]

The severity of this winter may be judged from the fact that one of these teamsters was drowned in a waterway, a sort of a slough, that crossed the road near where Frank Dowdy lives on the road between San Juan and Sargent.   The unfortunate driver had unhitched his team from the wagon driving them to town when he was caught in the torrent of water in this waterway, and it is thought that one of the horses must have kicked him in the struggle to get on the other side of the bank.   The body was afterwards found in the willows near the bridge.   Four of the New Idria six-horse teams were mired down in the turn of the road leading into the "Lane," coming from Hollister.   They hired Abner Moore, who had four yoke of oxen, and he managed to pull them out of the mire.   The condition of the rain-soaked ground was best evidenced by the fact that in pulling those teams that mired down, the wheels actually failed to turn and left small gulleys in the road which were filled with water for the remainder of the winter.

During this wet winter the only way that the New Idria Mines could be reached was to go up through the San Juan Canyon, passing where the cement plant is now located, turn left around a small hill, then through Flint's field toward the eastern end of the lane where you had to turn to the right and go through the low hills to New Idria.   It sometimes took three days for the teams to drive these four miles through Flint's fields.

The San Juan creek was so high that it washed out the old dam that had been constructed when the Mission was built and carried sand over a part of my father's place.   John Breen's ranch was covered partly with sand, and partly covered with water until late in the summer.   There were thousands of ducks there, and standing on the corner of my father's ranch in the evening I could shoot all the ducks I wanted.

Looking after some cattle on the north side of the Pajaro River, I was rained in for two weeks on the Pescadero at the Butterfield home.   I then crossed at what is now Sargent's Station.   John Woods, (a son of A. C. Woods and brother of Hy Woods, afterwards the prominent Watsonville building contractor), had a small boat in which he carried me over. With the aid of a long rope I led my horse behind me and made him swim across.   In crossing the San Benito, however, I got into the quicksand and came nearly being drowned.   The San Benito river in those days was not nearly as wide as it is today, but that flood and subsequent rainy seasons cut into the banks and carried away hundreds of acres of land.

The year 1862-1863 were very good years but in 1863-1864 there was but little rain, and the country in that section of Monterey County, as well as the lower end of Santa Clara County was covered with cattle, grazing throughout the range.   However, in the spring of 1864, with little rainfall, there was no new grass and the cattle having closely cropped the ground of the previous season's verdure, they commenced to starve and die.   My father and brother, Enoch, had about 135 head of cattle that ran at large.   My brother who did not care to go to school—in fact, he could not be hired to go— commenced to trade in cattle at the age of 15 years.   He bought and sold and took the first steps towards getting into the cattle business.

The 135 head of cattle that they owned were sold by my father and brother to Henry Miller.   They were delivered to Miller's men in the bed of the San Benito river, near the place where the bridge crosses the San Benito river.   Miller paid $2.50 a head for this bunch of cattle.   It was either take his terms or lose the stock.

Day after day droves of cattle would pass our house being driven to the "mantanza" (slaughter house) near Monterey, where the cattle were killed for their hides and horns.   The carcasses of the beeves were cooked in large kettles or cauldrons and fed to hogs.   Many of the poor beasts on their journey towards the slaughter house would fall in their tracks, to never get up, and were abandoned by their drivers.   Carcasses could be seen everywhere and the air was filled with the stench of the putrifying carcasses.

On the Pacheco ranch, which took in all that portion of what is now known as the Santa Ana Valley and the San Felipe section, there was a slough that lead into Soap Lake. This slough would be lined with the decaying carcasses of cattle who, too weak to pull themselves out of the mud, died there.   They died, by the hundreds, whilst striving to reach some tule, or some wisp of grass, that they saw growing on the banks of the slough.

Two firms located in Watsonville would make trips to the Pacheco section buying the hides.   One firm, Wise & Company, would make their round of the ranches the first part of the week, and the other firm, Friedlander & Company, would make their trip the latter part of the week.   They would carry on their trips a miscellaneous assortment of merchandise which they would exchange for hides.   Returning from these trading trips the big wagons of these firms would be seen loaded down with hides which towered high above the sides of the vehicle.

The driest year I ever saw in California was that of 1864.

It was in January, 1864, that the railroad reached San Jose and a big celebration in honor of the event was held. Many of the San Juan people attended this affair.   In March of that year my father went to San Francisco, following his annual custom of going to that city once a year to lay in provisions and household necessities for the following year. Also to purchase the outfit for setting up a repair shop wherein to repair guns, pistols and other articles.

I wanted to see the railroad and he took me along with him on this trip. My father, like myself, had never rode on a railroad. It was a great wonder to both of us, and I looked over the locomotive and cars very carefully. The locomotive appeared to me as a gigantic monster, which impression was deepened by the towering smoke-stack, the top of which was covered with wire as a spark arrester. In those days wood was the fuel and sparks were likely to set fire to the crops along the railroad's right-of-way.

It was a great sight to me. The trip was a revelation. I could scarcely contain myself but continually was putting my head out of the window watching that engine going along in front, and I was, constantly, pulling in my head with cinders in my eyes. One can imagine how I strutted around, when I got home, and told my wondering friends of my great trip.

I told my mother I wasn't feeling well and after she took a look at my tongue and the whites of my eyes, she ordered me to bed and with tea made from some of her medicinal herbs I soon developed a beautiful case of measles. The date I will always remember, March 29th. It was my birthday when I received that beautiful present.

Notwithstanding that 1864 was a "dry year" my father had a large crop of hay, owing to the fact that the biggest portion of the land that he owned was what is known as "wet land." He sold all his stock with the exception of fifteen cows and six horses. That season he sold to "Nigger Bill," the club-footed darkey teamster known throughout that section from San Jose to New Idria, twenty tons of loose clover and oat hay at twenty dollars a ton. Bill paid four hundred dollars for the hay just as it stood in the stack. "Nigger Bill" teamed between Alviso and the New Idria mines with a six-horse team.

CHAPTER XXI

The religious wave that struck San Juan in 1864—Abraham Lincoln's assassination—The story of Evans James ("Johnny Bull")

IT WAS in 1864 that San Juan was struck with a "religious fever."

The Baptists had a church erected on Monterey Street, close to the cemetery, opposite the old school house. As this church boasted a bell, with rope attached, the pupils used to ring the bell to summon the scholars to school.

Sometimes some of the boys would pull the bell cord so hard that it would turn the bell over, and it could not be rung at all. Then it became necessary for someone to climb into the belfry and release the bell, this being a rather hard task. I do not care to mention the names of the boys that were charged with the offense of turning the bell over, but as I frequently heard the names of Lupe Anzar, Fielding Hodges and Fernando Zanetta mentioned when any sort of mischief was done around the school, I am inclined to think they were the culprits; in fact, they would have to present me with a copper-riveted affidavit of denial, to alter my belief in this matter.

The Methodists built their church on Second and Church Streets. In former days there was but one Methodist church, but when the Civil War broke out that church divided into two denominations. The Methodist Church South, comprising Methodists who lived south of the Mason-Dixon line, and the Methodist Church comprised those residing north of that famous imaginary line. Akin to all communities in the United States, the San Juan Methodists divided and the North Methodists erected a building near the cemetery, on Church Street, and then commenced a series of revival meetings, that, for the time, took sole possession of public attention. Besides this religious outbreak there were camp-meetings in the willow grove over near old Gilroy. There were many baptisms in the Pajaro river, at its junction with the San Benito river. These baptisms were largely attended, especially by the younger element. I seldom missed one of them. The revival meetings were also a great attraction for us young fellows, for it was at the revival meetings that we had the privilege of taking the girls home, after services.

As is usual in such cases, as time went on, this wave of religion died out. The churches were deserted, and moved away —all except the Baptist church which was afterwards moved to the west side of Third Street, between Polk and Mokelumne Streets, where it now stands.

On the fourteenth of April, in the year 1865, one of the saddest events in history occurred. Abraham Lincoln was assassinated.

Such a calamity had never occurred before in the United States. It was no wonder that grief was shown on every side. He (Abraham Lincoln) had been a father to the people. In him was vested the rule and safeguard of the people. At this time, when a wise head and a pure heart was needed, he led us through the uncertain sands of statecraft.

I had the greatest respect for Abraham Lincoln, born in Kentucky, as was my father, and although father was a strong Democrat he voted for Lincoln. My father always claimed that if Lincoln had not been killed he would have brought order out of chaos and there never would have been such a cry as the "bloody shirt."

There being a large territory of grazing land in and about the Panoche Valley and Coalinga, many engaged in the cattle and sheep-raising business. That section being government land, no rental was charged on it, and the feed was free. These plainsmen, with their families, lived in San Juan. Some of these men I will mention as near as I can remember.   There was Russell & Reynolds, N. Crooks, Chas. Mitchell, Chas. Goodrich, Albion Baker, "Billy" Woods, Geo. W. McConnell and others.

As sheep were valuable at the time, and commanded good prices, the income of these sheepmen was spent in San Juan— they spent money freely, too, as also did the cattlemen and stock-buyers who came to town to purchase cattle.   As a consequence money circulated freely, and times in San Juan were booming.

One of the most prominent sheep buyers at that time was Evans James, known far and wide throughout the Monterey county as "Johnny Bull."   Evans was a large buyer and drove many herds to San Francisco.   James' reputation for honesty was so well established that it was not necessary for him to carry money with him wherewith to make purchases.   If he accepted the cattle at the price demanded and did not have the money to pay for the stock, it was all right.   James was merely told to take the cattle with him, and sometimes he would not be able to return for weeks.   No one that ever had any dealings with him had any misgivings as to being treated square by him. His modus operandi was simple.   Say he bought a flock of sheep at Tres Pinos, or further south, he would start with his flock for San Francisco driving them slowly and letting them feed off the grass on the way.   His care was such that by the time the mutton sheep reached San Francisco they were in prime condition.

It mattered nothing to "Johnny Bull" where night overtook him.   He would post his faithful shepherd dog over his flock, partake of supper, which consisted of crackers and cheese, and then wrapping himself in a blanket would lie down on the ground to sleep.

I remember that much amusement was occasioned on the return of Rafael Hernandez from one of those trips to San Francisco.   Rafael was hired by "Johnny Bull" to assist him in the drive, and when Rafael returned to San Juan he declared with many "carambas," and ejaculations of disgust that, under no circumstances would he ever again be caught on one of those trips with "Johnny Bull." During the trip, he solemnly declared, he had been given nothing to eat but hog beef and cracks! —meaning bacon and crackers which he could not easily translate into pure English.

By dint of industry and perseverance, in a few years "Johnny Bull" owned a fine ranch in the San Juan Valley and also had an excellent stock ranch near Hernandez, in southern San Benito County.

But adversity overtook the old fellow, and bad investments reduced him to penury. He lost all he possessed except a wagon and four mules. With this outfit he used to team, here and there, pursuing the same tactics that he employed whilst driving the sheep, viz: lie down beneath the stars at night wherever night's shadows overtook him, and let the mules graze on the surrounding verdure.

In May, 1866 I received the severest jolt that I ever had in my life. This was the death of my beloved mother. It changed the whole course of my life. My father, who had relied greatly on her wise counsel, was like a ship without a rudder on a trackless ocean. He had consulted my mother in regard to business matters and followed her advice implicitly, as she had the most executive ability of the two. Our hitherto happy home was like a bee hive without the queen bee.

This bereavement cost me dearly. My mother had patiently and laboriously saved up money enough to send me to college—a boon that I craved. Had she not died I would have been a much different man.

Elsewhere in these memoirs I have mentioned the disastrous fire that destroyed a number of blocks on Third Street. This fire occurred in 1867.

Sometime in 1866, Jas. Roache opened a merchandise store on the west corner of Second and Tuolumne Streets.

CHAPTER XXII

The great smallpox epidemic of 1868—Pitiful scenes—The town was quarantined by neighboring communities—The pest-house on the banks of the San Benito River

IN 1868 came the great epidemic that struck San Juan and all the surrounding districts sorely—it was the year of the great smallpox epidemic.

A wayfarer, coming from Los Angeles, put up for the night at the National Hotel. It was then conducted by Geo. Pullen, grandfather of Frank Pullen, of Watsonville. The man was sick, and Mr. Pullen called in a doctor who pronounced the man's affliction, measles.

San Juan citizens, always sympathetic, heard of this sick stranger and a number of them visited him, and tendered their services to help. Finally, James Collins, a man who had had the smallpox, went to call on this stranger, and when he looked at the man he remarked: "If that man hasn't got smallpox then I never had it." Collins was badly pock-marked from the ravages of the disease when it had attacked him in early youth. Those who had visited the stranger, in a few days, came down with the disease and the epidemic broke out all over the town.

There happened to be a big dance in town at this time, and a number of those stricken with the disease attended the dance, notwithstanding that they had a high fever. Of course, they thought it was some simple ailment that was troubling them. It was afterwards said that over forty that attended that dance came down with the disease in a few days.

And then a general hegira began. Some families taking, for the present, what simple necessities would do them, struck out for the mountains and camped there.

A pest house was erected by the citizens of San Juan on the banks of the San Benito river, near where Ben Flint's home stands now. The unfortunate victims of the disease who had no one to care for them were sent to this lonely spot. The disease proved to be of the most malignant type. Nurses could not be obtained anywhere, although as high as twenty dollars a night was offered them.

San Juan was quarantined on all sides. The roads leading to and from it were barred.

This disease extended to Watsonville where it carried off many victims. Watsonville, at one time, was as sorely stricken as San Juan. It was at the heighth of this epidemic that some panic-stricken citizens of Santa Cruz wrecked the bridge leading into the county seat, across Aptos creek. This was to prevent anyone from Watsonville coming into Santa Cruz. Their precaution was useless, however, for a few days afterward they had a dozen cases. This incident awoke great resentment among the people of Watsonville towards the people of Santa Cruz, and even to this day old-timers will bitterly revert to this incident.

San Juan was in sore straits. The stock of provisions was rapidly decreasing, and as no one was allowed to enter the town, or go out of it, the people were desperate. It is related that two of the citizens sneaked out and made their way to Monterey. On the outskirts of that settlement they changed their clothes and then went into that town to solicit aid and assistance for the stricken people of San Juan.

One of the men that went on this errand of mercy was George Pullen, a young lad, afterwards the father of Frank Pullen, of Watsonville. When these two men were recognized in Monterey everybody ran away from them, and it was only after a kind-hearted doctor took them in hand, heard heir story, and what they had done, that confidence was restored to the

Montereyans to the effect that the visitors were all right. Pullen and his associate returned with both money and provisions. The Montereyans had been exceedingly generous.

During this epidemic the dead were buried at night. Men were employed to dig the graves as fast as they could. I remember hearing that there were thirteen burials in one night, and after the epidemic was over it was reported that upwards of one hundred and thirty had died from the disease.

At the pest house James Collins and Joe Beals were in charge of the patients, and it was alleged that they drank heavily in order to ward off the disease. It is scarcely fair to blame them for this as the work they had to perform and the sights they saw was enough to drive any man to strong drink.

It is related, that one day, needing the bunk occupied by a certain patient who was very low, they decided that inasmuch as the man was due to die anyway he might as well die outside of the building as inside, accordingly, they picked the helpless patient up, carried him outside, and laid him on a slab where he reposed all night. The night was bitterly cold, but, strange to say, this man got well and the patient to whom they gave his bed, died.

The dead were hauled to the cemetery in a dump cart, and had to cross the San Juan creek; there was no bridge across the creek. On crossing this creek, one night, the corpse slipped out of the cart whilst the vehicle was going up the steep bank and the attendants did not miss the body until they got to the cemetery, whereupon they retraced their steps and brought back the corpse to its last resting place.

During the smallpox epidemic in 1868 I was attending Santa Clara College. It was in October of that year, just before I came home at the end of the school year, that the great earthquake occurred. Previously there had been slight earthquakes throughout California, but no extensive damage was done until this 'quake in October, 1868.

In common with the rest of the scholars I had to follow the usual custom of attending chapel services, and that morning I attended the services in the college chapel. A few minutes after I came out of the chapel an earthquake occurred.

It was a peculiar temblor in this: That the earth seemed to roll in waves. You could see trees swaying to and fro and the violence of the shock threw me to the ground. However, connected with the 'quake was a circumstance which tends to make one believe in fatalism—that is, when your time comes to cross the divide there is no use of endeavoring to escape the decree.

Overhanging the seat that I always occupied in the chapel was an immense glass chandelier. This chandelier weighed fully two hundred pounds. It was composed of myriads of gas jets and was adorned with hundreds upon hundreds of beautiful glass pendants hanging down, which, when the chandelier was lit, presented a dazzling effect This chandelier was shook from its fastenings and crashed down, smashing to pieces on the very seat that I always occupied at morning services. I often looked back on this happening, and wondered what strange providence was watching over me.

The chapel of the college was rent in twain diagonally, from one end of the roof to the other. San Jose suffered greatly in this earthquake; but, strange to say San Juan escaped with comparatively little damage, in fact, that great earthquake—for it was the greatest earthquake that had hitherto been experienced by the Yankees who were rapidly settling up California, was not nearly as severe to the Mission San Juan as was the quake of 1880 which leveled to the ground the brick end of the sisters' orphanage at the old mission, exposing both floors of the building at the end. Near where the brick wall fell out could be seen the dormitories of the little orphans with the neat small cots therein.

CHAPTER XXIII

*How the town of Hollister was started—San Benito County
created—County Seat should have been San Juan—The
man who said too many towns were named after saints*

GITATION in 1868, commenced to ferment, to a
certain extent, about creating a new county out of a
portion of Monterey county. It was spoken of
here and there but in the rush and hurly-burly do-
ings of the day but little was thought of it, and it was given
scant attention. However, in the minds of certain prominent
men of that section the idea was a very live issue and accordingly Col. Hollister started in to lay out the present city of Hollister.

It will be remembered, as is related in another portion of
these memoirs, that, originally, the Flint-Bixby Company and
Col. Hollister formed a partnership and purchased from Don
Pacheco the San Justo grant. Sometime after that purchase this
partnership was dissolved and the San Justo grant was divided
between the Flint-Bixby Company and Col. Hollister, the
latter taking the eastern portion of the grant and the Flint-
Bixby Company taking the western portion of the ranch, and
paying Hollister a bonus of $10,000 therefor.

In 1868 Col. Hollister, with a number of other prominent
men in that section, formed what was known as the "San Justo
Homestead Association." [20] This association was duly incorpor-
ated. The object in forming the association was to divide
this portion of the San Justo grant into farms and sell them to
farmers, also to establish a town for the convenience of the
purchasers of the land. This idea of locating a town was used
as a means of selling the lands. Nearly everyone in that section,
at that time, were farmers and the idea of acquiring some of
these lands found favor.

The association announced that this land was to be divided into farms and grazing lots. There were to be fifty-one lots, the fifty-first lot was to be dedicated as a town site. These lots, or parcels of land as they were called, were sold at auction, the highest premium taking the first choice, which went to pay on the purchase.

The late Thos. Hawkins, the Hollister banker, purchased the first choice which cost him upwards $6,000. That sum was considered an enormous price, but as matters developed eventually it showed Hawkins' good judgment and served to justify the confidence bestowed upon that good man in later years.

Tom Hawkins, afterwards the most prominent citizen of San Benito county, had come there in early days and had worked as a laborer on various projects, principally on hay baling and grain threshing outfits. At the time that he made this purchase great was the surprise that he, by his patience and thrift, had accumulated such a sum. *

There was spirited bidding on the lots and all were sold. The town of Hollister was laid out in November, 1868. At a

---

* EDITOR'S NOTE—The memory of the late Thos. S. Hawkins will ever be held in grateful remembrance by the editor of the Pajaronian. A finer and better man we have never met. The mention of his purchase of this property above, reminds us of a talk we had with him one day in his bank. On this occasion Tom was somewhat reminiscent. He owned the finest home in all San Benito county, a beautiful block in which his residence was embowered in plants and flowers. On the occasion which we refer to he told us of his early struggles when he came to Hollister and how hard he worked with a threshing outfit. He said, "Myself and my wife occupied a little shack on the other side of what is now called San Benito street and outside of the stove, which I managed to buy in San Francisco, all the furniture in the house was made by myself after working hours. Our bed was nailed to the side of the wall, and was constructed of rough boards. We slept on a tick full of straw. I made the table for the kitchen and I made four chairs out of four barrels that I managed to secure.

"Looking back I consider that the chairs that I manufactured were somewhat ingenious as I cut a section out of one side and Mrs. Hawkins, who was very clever, stuffed the back, sides and seat with straw. They were, indeed, very comfortable. Do you know that some days, looking backwards, notwithstanding the fact that I have such a beautiful home meeting of the association it was decided to place the town site about a mile and a half northeast of its present location inasmuch as Hollister had reserved, for himself, a homestead taking in a portion of the present town site, however, after considerable discussion, the idea was abandoned and it was decided to place the town on the site that it now occupies.

At a meeting it was proposed by someone to call the town "San Justo." But, a man by the name of Hagen, who was present, arose and vigorously denounced the proposition, saying that he would be blankety-blanked if they called that town by any "San," that he was tired of running across "San" attached to every town that he surveyed—San Juan, San Jose, San Luis Obispo, etc. After talking the matter over it was decided, by the association, to call the town after Col. Hollister. [21]

Col. Hollister in 1862 had built, what was considered in those days a fine residence, on Fourth Street opposite where the present court house now stands. Connected with the residence he had many corrals, sheep pens, and a long string of water troughs lining the roadway in front of his premises. He also built a large barn which was afterwards occupied by Jim Hodges as a livery stable.

---

at the present time, I verily believe that I never had so much fun and enjoyed life so thoroughly as when I occupied that shack in company with my wife and family."

Thos. Hawkins' remarks brought a reminiscence to our mind of a similar remark being made by Bill Carson, one of the lumber kings of Eureka, Humboldt county. Bill Carson built a mansion at the head of Second street that is one of the sights of Eureka; it is two stories in heighth and contained all modern conveniences even to a commodious billiard room. When he concluded to erect this home he sent to Switzerland and brought from that country one of its leading wood carvers. He put the man to work making the carvings for the house and it took the man several years to complete the task. When the job was finished Carson offered $5,000 reward to anyone that would show him two pieces of carving alike on the structure. Alongside this beautiful mansion, covered with ivy was a log cabin, the original home of Mr. and Mrs. Carson when they came to Eureka. This log cabin was carefully preserved and left in exactly the same condition that it was the day they forsook it and took up their residence in the big mansion adjoining. Whenever Carson was found missing, a search would reveal the old man smoking in the cabin and he often declared that he had better times in the log cabin than he ever enjoyed in the grand home.—Ed. Pajaronian.

The Hollister residence was, years afterwards, made into a hotel—the only hotel in that section, outside of San Juan—and was called the Montgomery House owing to the fact that it was conducted by a man by the name of Montgomery.   Mr. Montgomery's son (Edward) years afterwards was treasurer of San Benito county.

The Montgomery House was very nicely located.   It had much shrubbery and trees about it and was a favorite resort for travelers going and coming.   Sometime around 1884-85 it caught fire from some unknown cause and was burned to the ground.   The land was afterwards purchased by the school district and a grammar and primary school erected thereon.

The first man to purchase town lots in the new city of Hollister was J. A. Owens.   He purchased two lots for $100 apiece.   The prices on the town lots were $100 for inside lots and $200 for corner lots.

Owens established the first store in Hollister.   C. W. Wentworth also opened a store and was afterwards appointed postmaster.

The town started off and began to grow rapidly.   The smallpox had worked great injury to San Juan.   Many of its inhabitants, becoming disheartened at the trials that they had undergone and the sad scenes that they witnessed, moved to Hollister, after buying lots in that town.

And now Gilroy, a little settlement, began to forge ahead, and, in 1869 the railroad reached this settlement and as it was the nearest point that the railroad could be reached, the travelers desiring to take the trains had to repair to that city.   Gilroy went rapidly ahead.   Prior to this Gilroy was anything but commercially important, but the railroad, making its terminus there, made it the distributing point for all sections south as far as San Luis Obispo, which town, owing to its water connection, did not need railroad facilities.

San Juan began to fail. Gilroy on the north was taking away her trade customers and Hollister on the southeast was also cutting in to her trade. The town began to decline. The loss can well be imagined when I state not only did she lose the trade connected with the seven stage lines that passed through her streets, but also the large trade that went through to the New Idria mines and way points. Gilroy was a very active town. Its streets were crowded with big teams loaded with hay and grain destined to be shipped by the railroad to points north. So these conditions continued until the railroad was built to Hollister, where it made its terminus for a long time, in fact, at that time there was a fifty-fifty bet that Hollister was on the main overland line of the railroad, for the company ran surveys from Hollister through Tres Pinos up the San Benito and cut across through Topo Valley heading for San Luis Obispo; but, in the meantime, Watsonville commenced to loom up as a big trade center and Salinas was building up as a big town, so finally the railroad company concluded to push its line on to Watsonville and thence over to Salinas and down through the Salinas Valley. One can hardly imagine what would have been the result to Hollister had the railroad's original plan not been abandoned. Some day that line will be put through by the railroad and strike the present line going down the Salinas Valley somewhere in the vicinity of King City. It is estimated that this route will cut off many miles necessitated now by the present detour around by way of Sargent station, Watsonville Junction and Salinas

This extension of the railroad to Hollister hurt Gilroy badly, and San Juan was completely "knocked out." Then regret circulated amongst the people, that they had not acceded to the proposal of the railroad company to build its line to San Juan after receiving a subsidy of $60,000 including a right of way. At that time San Juan's principal property owners were sheep and cattle men and they opposed this proposition vigorously, stating that inasmuch as it was only a few miles to Gilroy they could drive their herds to that point and thus save the $60,000 asked by the railroad company. It was a fatal mistake from which both San Juan and Watsonville, (who also refused to give any subsidy) are still suffering.

San Juan had suffered from the disastrous fire that I have referred to elsewhere; the awful smallpox epidemic; and now, the railroad taking its trade away to Hollister, despair settled upon the community which despair was accentuated when a number of its prominent merchants commenced to move their stocks to Hollister and start business there.

In 1870 Hollister had a population of about two hundred, and its growth can be judged from the fact that in 1873 a census of its population showed two thousand inhabitants.

CHAPTER XXIV

County division and how it was brought about—How the
boundary line was gerrymandered—Division lost out at
the first election but was carried at the next election

IN 1871-72 Monterey county was in the throes of a
fight over the removal of its county seat. It will
be remembered that the county seat at that time was
Monterey, and a proposition was broached to move
the county seat to a more central location in that big county.

Castroville at the news that the county seat might be
moved commenced to perk up. Juan B. Castro, after whom the
town was named, laid the town out in lots, and in order to
induce people to settle there would offer them a lot free if they
would agree to build on it, the idea being to make it such a
populous center that it could carry off the county seat at the
proposed election.

Salinas, then a small settlement, commenced to take stock,
and it also got into the fight.

Then, to add to the turmoil and general unrest, Hollister
started a fight for county division; that is, its residents wanted
that portion of Monterey set aside and made into a new county.
The excitement throughout Monterey county began to grow.
There were plenty of things to excite men. Here was a proposition not only to divide the county, but also to move the
county seat away from Monterey.

There were able gerrymanderers on both sides and through
some hokus-pokus a line was run from what was then known
as the Aromas Valley straight over Fremont's Peak leaving out
the Carneros section, wherein lived quite a number of inhabitants that always traded in San Juan; and also left out the
Pajaro Valley, which earnestly desired to be included within
the confines of the proposed new county.

Hollister had nothing to fear after the line was drawn, she would either have all or nothing. So the fight started and no stone was left unturned to accomplish the division of the county.

The election of an essemblyman to the legislature hinged on this county division, and this caused politics to loom up in the fight. Both Democrats and Republicans forgot all partisanship and would hob-nob and connive with each other.

At the first election the divisionists lost; but, undismayed those who wanted division girded up their loins, buckled on their armor, and went into the fight for division again.

To show the intense feeling which existed at that time, at one of the elections held, that grand old man of Monterey county, the late Hon. J. R. Hebron, who was an anti-divisionist, was nominated for assemblyman. Hebron was one of the leading men in Monterey county, a man of irreproachable character; his standing as a man and as a citizen was unquestionable. In running for the office of assemblyman he received, out of several hundred votes cast, only eight votes on the San Juan-Hollister side.

Those interested in dividing Monterey county, notwithstanding that they had lost the first election, did not relax their efforts throughout the two ensuing years, and at the next election by superior political tactics, generalship, and, it was also rumored, by the free use of money and promises, succeeded in electing their man to represent the county in the assembly. He squeezed through by a small majority.

This brought the project, or, we might say, contest, of dividing the county, up to the legislature, but the fight did not end there. The introduction of the bill to divide Monterey county into the legislature, precipitated a hot fight. The bill was introduced first in the assembly, and then introduced into the senate, and the warring factions tossed the bill back and forth several times. However, the divisionists, by a hard fight, succeeded in getting the measure through and Monterey county lost the fairest portion of its territory. After it passed the assembly the senate approved the measure by a bare majority.

Then the divisionists commenced to rejoice, but their rejoicing proved to be somewhat premature, as Governor Newton Booth held the bill up. The members of the "Third House" made the life of the governor miserable by their insistent demand that he veto the bill. However, the mass of figures and facts presented in favor of the divisionists could not be gainsayed and finally Governor Booth signed the bill on the twelfth of February, 1874, and San Benito county was created.

No credit could be attached to anyone in particular, for the sentiment in favor of division was so wide-spread and universal in this section that all the settlers in the region affected, voted as one man.

Under the "act" creating the new county Governor Booth appointed five commissioners who were charged with the organization of this new county. The commissioners were Thos. S. Hawkins, Jess Whitton, Mark Pomeroy, John Breen and H. M. Hayes.

A few days after their appointment by the governor, this commission met and organized by electing John Breen as president and H. M. Hayes as secretary.

The commission proceeded to business and divided the county into four townships, namely; Hollister, San Juan, Paicines and San Benito. The supervisorial districts were: Hollister number one; San Juan number two; Paicines and San Benito number three.

The county officers were appointed by the governor to hold office until the special election on March 26, 1874. The county seat was to be located by popular vote. The officers elected were: Benj. F. Ross, sheriff and ex-official tax collector; H. M. Hayes, county clerk and recorder; N. C. Briggs, district attorney; Thos. McMahon, treasurer; Haydon Dowdy, assessor;

Frank P. McCray, surveyor; H. C. Morris, superintendent of schools and J. M. Black, coroner and public administrator. Jas. F. Breen, county judge of Monterey county, resigned that position and was appointed by the governor as county judge of San Benito county. [22]

The supervisors elected were: District number one, Mark Pomeroy; district number two, Thos. Flint; and district number three, D. J. Watson.

There was quite a difference between Monterey and the newly created county of San Benito over the matter of the debt of Monterey county. Monterey county had quite a debt hanging over it, and, of course, a certain proportion of that debt San Benito county had to pay. An "act" to settle the differences between the two counties was passed by the legislature, but after its passage it was found that it would not solve the difficulty, so the "act" was amended, and under its provisions the Board of Supervisors, of each county, met jointly, and selected a commission of five members to arbitrate the matter. Two of the committeemen were named by San Benito county, two named by Monterey county and the third was named by the judge of the twentieth judicial district.

The committee met in session at Salinas, and after examining the books of that county found that Monterey county was in debt, and that of this debt there was chargeable to San Benito county a little over $5,800. To meet this indebtedness five year bonds were issued at seven percent interest, payable to Monterey county or order. Accordingly, San Benito county started out with a debt on its taxpayers.

It will be remembered that in 1872 the subject of dividing Monterey county and creating a new county out of its western portion was being agitated and was defeated at the election in 1872. This was owing to the fact that there were so many issues before the people; for, be it remembered a big agitation was going on in Monterey county over the removal of the county seat from Monterey.

Now, logically, the county seat should be in the center of the county, or as near as possible to the center of a county. There were three contestants in the fight for the county seat of Monterey county, namely: Monterey, Castroville, and Salinas. Amidst all the pulling and hauling in this county seat matter, in Monterey county, there was not so much attention paid to the county division issue.   Consequently, in the 1872 election, the county division issue was defeated, and Salinas was selected as the future county seat of Monterey county.

As mentioned before, in these memoirs, the proponents for county division were not idle during the ensuing two years and in the discussion of the proposed division of Monterey county it was learned that the Pajaro Valley, disgusted with not having decent roads leading to and from that place, was willing to come in to the new county.   If the Pajaro Valley was taken in and made a part thereof, San Juan would be selected as the county seat, being the nearest to the center of the proposed new county.

The idea of making San Juan the county seat did not meet with the approval of the Hollister folks.   The chief objection in their minds, in regard to the division matter, was to secure the county seat for Hollister.   Accordingly, Monterey county was tipped off as to the desires of the Pajaro valley people to come into the new county and the Montereyans thereupon declared that, under no circumstances, would they sacrifice that section of the county inasmuch as it promised to be the richest section around Monterey bay.   So, when the division lines were drawn the Hollister folks cunningly contrived to place the division lines between Monterey and the new county, where they are at present.   The line extended through the center of Aromas and thereby eliminated all possible chances of San Juan becoming the county seat, because it was located too near the lower end of the new county.   Then Hollister felt that by running the line along the Pajaro river and then in a direct line to the top of Fremont peak, thus giving Monterey the Carneros section which, at that time, contained a large population, it would help to placate Monterey's animosity against the division scheme, and would insure the county seat being located at or near Hollister. But, another rival for the county seat appeared in Paicines. It was held, and logically too, that Paicines was nearer the center of the new county than was Hollister. However, when the vote came up, Hollister carried away the prize by virtue of its large population, and San Juan and Paicines were left out in the cold. Out of this county seat matter there grew an intense animosity against Hollister—a bitter feeling that exists to the present day, especially amongst the older generation. The San Juan people felt, for years, that they had been unjustly treated in the county seat matter by the people of Hollister. They claimed, and with great justice too, that their town site was far superior to that of Hollister; that it had a finer climate; was closer to the main line of travel both by railroad and highway; was known all over the country as one of the oldest towns in California, and that its many claims should have been recognized by adding Pajaro Valley to the new county and then placing the county seat at San Juan.

CHAPTER XXV

The early newspapers of San Benito County—Rapid growth
of Hollister—It becomes a great mart for
fine horses and grain

HE WEEKLY Hollister Enterprise was established by the late John McGonigle. Its first issue was in October, 1873, and its last in January 1881, when it merged into a paper called "The Pacific Coast."

After many vicissitudes the Pacific Coast was merged into the Hollister Free Lance and after that the Farmer's Alliance started a paper known as the West Coast Alliance which ultimately was taken over by several Democrats and renamed the Hollister Bee.

Under McGonigle's control the Enterprise was the best local paper ever published in the county. It was always foremost for the advancement of Hollister and vicinity. Eventually McGonigle went to Ventura and started the Ventura Democrat which he conducted for years. He, under Cleveland's administration, was appointed collector of the port at that place.

After his death the paper was bought and renamed the Ventura Post and a year or so ago was merged into the Ventura Star.

John McGonigle was one of the ablest editors on the Pacific coast. He was an Irish-Missourian and was Democratic to the backbone.

The next weekly newspaper started in the new county of San Benito was the Advance, published by a veteran newspaper man by the name of Shaw. Shaw, who was a relative of the famous writer, George Bernard Shaw, had a large family of boys and one daughter. The Shaw boys in after years played a conspicuous part in the development of San Benito county.

There were five papers published in San Juan; the first paper that I remember was the "Central Californian," which was published by Bryerly & Clevenger, in 1869. The next paper to be launched on the journalistic sea was the "San Juan Echo," published by A. D. Jones in 1870. In 1880 a school paper was published, but when the school closed the paper was discontinued. "The San Juan Enterprise" was published in 1893 by Gates & Baptist and the last paper was "The Missing Link" published by J. W. Thomas in 1899.

The present ably conducted paper, "The San Juan Mission News" has had a longer life than any paper ever started at San Juan. It is a splendid weekly, and reflects credit upon its town.

Thos. Beck, of Watsonville, was at the time of the division of the county, senator-elect from Monterey and Santa Cruz counties and had quite a say in the creation of the new county.[23]

After the creation of San Benito county, Hollister began to grow, and in time became a very flourishing town. Being of virgin soil, the farmers in that county produced immense crops of hay, wheat and barley. The hay was always of top-notch quality, and today, is considered second to none in the state.

Large warehouses were built in Hollister and filled with wheat, barley and hay.

Hollister also became noted for the good horses and fine stock raised in that section. The farmers were breeding large draft horses and fine carriage horses. Some of the finest six-horse teams in the state could be seen day after day drawing immense loads of hay, grain and barley to the warehouses. Many other teams could be seen standing in line waiting their turn to be unloaded. It was a great place where horse buyers from San Francisco and other parts of the state repaired to acquire both horses and stock.

One of the most prominent horse traders as well as horse breeders in that section was Len Ladd, whose extensive ranch was about a mile, or a mile and a half, outside of town. If a call was made for a matched team of horses for draying purposes, for a hearse or a carriage, in fact, any driving purpose, Len Ladd was the man who could supply them at a moment's notice.

A flour mill was built by J. M. "Baldy" Brown in 1870. "Baldy," in 1879, sold out this business to Dick Shakelford and a man by the name of Hinds.   The flour mill's product under "Baldy" Brown did not amount to much.   Shakelford and Hinds reconstructed the mill and turned out flour that became statewide in its reputation for good quality.

Shakelford afterwards went to Templeton and became one of the founders of that town.

Joaquin Bolado, who came into the county in 1867, had bought some 10,000 acres of land in the Santa Ana and Tres Pinos district sub-divided it into small tracts and sold it to farmers.   This land produced good crops of hay and grain. Fairview also had been purchased by farmers, and the threshing machine whistle could be heard blowing at Hollister from various points of the compass.

ROZAS' FRAME HOUSE, BUILT 1856

CHAPTER XXVI

The author's marriage lasted, happily, for forty-one years—
The dry year of 1877—Hundreds of families migrating—
Poor prices for stock—The trade dollar

HE POET says that : "In the spring a young man's fancy lightly turns to thoughts of love." But this was not my case.

In the fall of 1876, shortly after coming out of Pleasant Valley, I persuaded the girl that I thought was the "ownliest one" in the world, Elizabeth Adelia Thorne to become my wife. You remember I mentioned, elsewhere, the little girl that I used to see and admire through the fence, playing in the yard of her grandparents, Ben and Mary Wilcox, at San Juan. I used to see this pretty little girl playing in the yard when I was going to, and coming from, school, and the romance that then began, in early days of my boyhood, culminated in her becoming my wife in 1876.

We were married in the parlor of the Western Hotel in Hollister. The hotel was then conducted by the Rector Bros., who, after conducting, for some time, the McMahon house in Hollister migrated to Grass Valley, where they became noted bonifaces of northern California. We were married on the fourth of December. My wife died, after having undergone an operation, in the Watsonville hospital, on January 31, 1918, after forty-one years of married life. We had four children: Edna, now Mrs. Ernest Sherwood, of Watsonville; Cora, now Mrs. R. D. Monroe. of Monterey, and our sons were Oscar, now living in Watsonville, and Earl, residing in Monterey.

As I have remarked before, 1877 was a dry year. To those who have never passed through a dry year, in the southern part of the state, the words "dry year" mean but little. But, to those afflicted by a shortage of feed and crops, the term "dry year" strikes terror.

The Pajaro Valley in that year produced some crops but San Benito county and in the southern part of the state the conditions were distressful owing to the drought.

I was, at the time of this drought, living in the Wilcox home at the end of The Alameda at the extension of Third street, San Juan, which led to the Salinas road. Having ten acres which contained a good well, on part of this tract I raised a fine vegetable garden. I was on the direct road from the southern travel going north, and in a position where I could see all the wagons passing, and, indeed, some days there were strings of them. These wagons generally consisted of people migrating from the south in search of better living conditions in the north. The wagons, usually of the covered type, were occupied by a driver and his family. In some other part of the state they had nailed up their home, and with hopeful resignation started out on this journey in search of some place where a living might be made. Most of these migratory families were folks who had taken up claims in southern Monterey or San Luis Obispo counties, or in counties further south. If any of these immigrants were asked where they were going, their reply would be indefinite—they had no place picked out.

You could sell nothing. I have seen a finely matched team, well broken, go begging for $40.

Arthur Graham, a butcher in San Juan, in partnership with the Flint-Bixby Co., rented my father's place and erected thereon some large kettles. Graham furnished the hogs and Flint-Bixby & Co., furnished the sheep to be slaughtered, for hog feed. The Flint-Bixby Co., figured that by killing the older sheep thus reducing the herds, and keeping only the young ones, that they could pull through the dry season, and so the slaughter commenced.

At the outset some of these sheep slaughtered were fairly good mutton. Some of the carcasses I bought at fifty cents a carcass. On Bird Creek was a man who had 2,000 goats. He killed them and sold them by the quarter. One day he delivered orders to Hollister, another day orders to San Juan, and so on. He charged 35c for a hind quarter and considerably less for a fore quarter. As an illustration of how hard it was to sell anything: I bought a 350-pound hog for three cents a pound, in other words I got the animal for $10.50.

There were also a number of families in the San Juan Valley who had considerable hay, but not enough to feed horses through the season and plow the ground for the coming year's crop. Some of these families combined, rented a large tract of land above Corralitos in the vicinity of Brown Valley and Corralitos creek, and, in this way, succeeded in pulling their horses through the season in fairly good shape. It cannot be said that the horses did well as the pasture was very scant, indeed, but they managed to live.

About this time California was flooded with trade dollars, a new coin that was minted for the Chinese trade and was intended to offset the Mexican dollar. These dollars were put into circulation in consequence of which gold was hoarded up, and, as the common payment in business circles was always gold, merchants were offering as high as a dollar premium for a $20 gold piece. On one occasion I got $22 for a twenty dollar gold piece. The stores had signs over their counters notifying the public that not over five dollars in silver would be accepted in trade. Silver dollars were at a big discount. This condition ran for three or four years, until, finally, the trade dollar disappeared.

To add to our misery, now and then, when business was at a standstill, we would have a panic. No one could borrow from the bank unless they had fluid security. I remember on on occasion, riding over to Hollister with Hayden Dowdy —Dowdy was the political boss for years, of San Benito county. He was re-elected, many terms, as assessor, and under Cleveland's administration he retired from the assessor's office and was appointed postmaster at Hollister. His son, Elmer Dowdy for the past twenty-six years has been county clerk, auditor, and recorder of that county. Hayden Dowdy, at the time that I am speaking of, owned a very fine farm in the San Juan Valley. This farm, which is still owned by his descendants, is considered one of the finest farms in the valley.

Riding along San Benito street, in Hollister, that day we passed the Bank of Hollister, whereupon Dowdy remarked, "Mylar, the country is pretty hard up. Do you know that I could not borrow two hundred dollars from that bank on my fine ranch."

In passing let me remark that we should hold in grateful remembrance the memory of Woodrow Wilson who gave us the reserve banks to stop any future panics. In looking over the record books in those days it was ascertained that over ninety per cent of the farms in San Benito county were mortgaged.

In 1878 there was no rain up to about the middle of January. The fall of 1878 had also been dry, and I, being afraid that another dry year was in prospect, made up my mind to go to some region where it would rain. With my wife and little baby, I set sail, via steamer, for Oregon. It was raining when we got there. I had an uncle living in Astoria, at the mouth of the Columbia river, and so we stopped with this relative. I had shipped up there all our household goods in large boxes, sending them to my uncle. When I unpacked the goods I was going to destroy the boxes but my uncle told me to save them. I inquired, "Why?" He merely told me that I might need them, and, accordingly, I put them away safely.

Soon after I procured a very good position from the government. But, it rained! and rained! and rained! I got a sou'-wester, a pair of rubbers, and a raincoat. My wife said that she could not dry the wash outside and so a rack had to be put in the kitchen for this purpose. Coming up, the voyage being stormy, my wife was dreadfully sea-sick, and on landing on terra firma declared that never would she go back to California until a railroad was built between the two states. But, in five months, she told me that she had had enough of rain to suit her for the rest of her life and that, if I was willing, she would start with me for California again.

So the packing boxes came in handy. My uncle proved to be wise unto his generation. I remember one day asking him if they ever had a dry day in Astoria, and he contemplatively looked out at the mouth of the Columbia river and answered, "Yes, we have three dry days in August every year!" Looking back over those days I cannot remember, during my stay there, of one single day that it did not rain sometime during the twenty-four hours.

So, buying a ticket from the steamship company, we returned to California and it certainly did look good to me when I once more reached it. I have never left it since.

MARK REGAN DRIVING CONCORD STAGE BUILT IN 1873

CHAPTER XXVII

Some of the notable characters in San Juan that the author remembers—Mark Regan, the noted stage driver—The disappearance of Senor Sanchez—Buried treasure

---

IN 1870 Jake Beuttler (the brewer) came to San Juan and located on the north side of Third Street. At this place he built a residence and a brewery. Beuttler, together with his stepson Fred Beck, manufactured a fine quality of beer. This beer was the favorite beverage in the central part of the coast counties. He also ran a four-horse delivery wagon through the San Joaquin Valley as far as Firebaugh's Ferry, on the San Joaquin river, which, in those days, was a very lively settlement. There were shearing pens at Firebaugh, in which, in shearing seasons, over 100,000 sheep were sheared. Beuttler had three childrern: George, Albert and Annie. Annie afterwards became the wife of the noted stage driver, Mark Regan—"the grand old man of the whip."

Mark Regan was a noted character, and did more to keep San Juan on the map than any other citizen that the town ever possessed. He ran the stage, for years from Sargent station, where it connected with the railroad, to San Juan, and Hollister. He never drank, smoked or gambled. He came originally from Pike's Peak during the gold rush.

In his day he carried more distinguished people over his stage route than any other driver in the state of California. Everyone knew Mark Regan, a man of infinite jest, and one of the greatest of story-tellers. To hear Mark describe the driving of the last spike at Promotory, Utah, connecting the two railroads, the Central Pacific and the Union Pacific, was a masterpiece of verbal description. Mark is authority for the statement that it was at the driving of the last spike that George Pullman got his idea for his Pullman sleeping cars.

It was a privilege much sought by travelers to occupy the front seat with Mark Regan, for, during the trip from Sargent station to Hollister he would regale the wayfarer with stories innumerable, and point out the many objects of interest embellishing them with tales that he had learned from the early San Juan pioneers and Indians.

Some time after the big fire in San Juan Mr. Giacoma, an Italian, started to erect a stone building on the west side of Third Street, between Polk and Mariposa Streets. It was built of sandstone taken from the adjacent hills, which stone was cut and shaped into blocks on the ground on which the building was to be erected. It took some time to complete this building and it was a losing proposition for Giacoma. It has been remodeled and additions added, since then, and for many years past has been owned by A. Taix. At one time, when San Juan was in the midst of one of its worst depressions, this stone building, notwithstanding the fact that it cost nearly $20,000 to erect, could have been purchased for $800. Since then it has been a valuable piece of property.

In 1872 Thos. McMahon moved his stock of merchandise to Hollister and located on the west side of San Benito Street, between Fourth and Fifth Streets. The removal of this merchandise store was another black eye for San Juan. At the same time other merchants were preparing to follow McMahon's example.

One of the noted characters in San Juan in its early days, before my father settled there, was Senor Sanchez, a very prominent Spaniard. There were, and still are, many stories extant about Sanchez. He was drowned whilst crossing the Pajaro river, near that river's junction with the San Benito river. The Sanchez' family residence was a large two-story adobe building located on the east side of the Pajaro river, a short distance above where the two rivers unite. [24]

One of the stories current, and it is related by many old-timers now, is that the night that Sanchez lost his life he had been in San Jose and had received a large amount of money, the weight of which caused his horse and himself to mire into the quicksand. Neither the horse nor the man were ever seen again.

Facing the Sanchez' home, on the east, was a hill. It was quite a large hill, and the rumor grew that Sanchez had buried an immense amount of gold dust and money in that hill. In consequence of this rumor every now and then people would repair to the hill and dig hither and thither, according to directions that they had received from fortune tellers. Some had divining rods to point out the buried gold, others depended upon plats and maps that were furnished, (for a consideration), by the fortune tellers. But, somehow or another, no money was ever found by the treasure seekers. It is worthy of note that, so far as I know, no San Juan people ever went to that hill to dig for the supposed buried treasure. Those who sought the gold were from San Jose, Watsonville, San Francisco and other parts of the state.

This reminds me of another supposed buried treasure in this section. In the early days two men were hung in the vicinity of the "San Juan Rocks," near Dunbarton. The rumor spread that the two men had buried some eight or ten thousand dollars in that neighborhood and some people are actually searching for that treasure yet. Another place that was extensively mined was the glass house that occupied a prominent place on the Salinas road on the site where the Watsonville golf club is now located. Buried treasure was supposed to be plentiful in that vicinity and many were the expeditions that set out to resurrect treasure trove.

However, soon after Sanchez disappeared, his family, searching for some of the treasure that they knew he possessed, found $1,300 in a barrel of beans, in the storeroom of the dwelling, and a great many persons believe that this amount represented all the money that Sanchez had.

After Sanchez' death, his widow married a Dr. Sanford, who subsequently was killed in the barroom of a Monterey hotel by parties who, it is said, were searching for this supposed treasure of Sanchez,' and that in the argument that ensued between these parties, and Sanford, Dr. Sanford was killed. After Sanford's death Mrs. Sanchez-Sanford married an attorney by the name of Geo. W. Crane.   Crane lived in San Juan and died during the smallpox epidemic in 1868.

In Watsonville, these stories of buried treasure around San Juan had been so magnified in the re-telling that some of the yarns were almost preposterous. Mr. Roache, a prominent citizen of Watsonville, whose body was found in a well, at the upper end of Main Street, was supposed to have been a victim of some of the parties searching for the Sanchez treasure: Roache, who was known throughout this section, was supposed to have been an amigo of Sanchez, and people thought that Sanchez had told him where he had put the money.   By "money" is meant principally gold dust, for in the latter fifties but little of the minted currency was in circulation.   The gold miners were digging the gold out of the creeks and gulches in northern California.   The gold dust and gold nuggets were the chief media of exchange.

San Juan, in the early '60's, boasted of a noted character in the person of Wm. Wiggins whom a great many people styled "Doctor."   Wiggins came to California from St. Louis, Missouri, in 1840.   His father at that time was the owner of the ferry across the Mississippi river at St. Louis.   A love of adventure prompted Wiggins, a young man, in 1839, to join a party of trappers on one of their expeditions.   The meanderings of this party of trappers finally led them to California.   Wiggins became interested in, and claimed an interest and ownership in, the New Almaden quicksilver mines, in Santa Clara county.   Litigation followed his claim, and he lost out, which prompted him to write home to his father for more money wherewith to press an appeal to the higher courts.

Wiggin's father refused to send him the money but settled a trust fund on the son, the interest of which provided him with a comfortable yearly annuity. This enabled him to live in comfort and he subsequently settled at the Plaza Hotel in San Juan, where he roomed and boarded for years. He was singular in this: He ate but two meals a day—breakfast at nine o'clock and dinner at five o'clock. He lived a gentleman's life. He was a rather small man in size, and wore a Prince Albert coat and a white hat which made him a distinctive person amongst the rest of San Juan's inhabitants. He pursued a regular routine. He would make a trip to Kemp's saloon in the forenoon and then another one in the afternoon and taking his place at one of the deserted card tables would play, day after day, solitaire. If asked to take a drink, unless the time was within a few minutes of his scheduled period wherein he "liquidated" his thirst each day, he would refuse the proffered courtesy. Two drinks a day was all he allowed himself; one in the forenoon and one in the afternoon.

JIM JACK (1900 NEWSPAPER CLIPPING)

CHAPTER XXVIII

Wages were low in 1878—Long hours were worked—Farmers
not doing well—Some old settlers—Tribute to "China
Jim," whose charity was unbounded

THE YEAR 1878 was a quiet but a good year as far as the farmers were concerned. However, there were thousands of idle men in the state. Wages were low. Farmers got all the help they wanted at $1.00 and $1.50 a day, with board, but the laborer had to furnish his own blankets and could sleep any place he liked. The working hours were from daylight until dark. The men driving teams had to look after their team and wagon on Sundays. That is, all necessary repairs were made on the wagon, and the horses had to be in prime condition for another week's work. This condition of affairs remained as long as the farmers raised grain. It would appear that from these conditions that the farmers should ere long become wealthy, but such was not the case. They were not doing any too well. Owing to the short seasons that came, and the fluctuation of prices, the average price of wheat, per cental, in 1864, and for twenty years thereafter, was around $1.60, and barley was a great deal lower than that. I remember one year when there was a good crop of barley raised in the San Juan section. One farmer had 15,000 sacks (100 pounds to the sack) of ripe, plump barley. This barley usually brought a good price for brewing purposes, but, this season, all that farmer was offered for his crop was fifty cents a cental, and out of this he had to subtract the price of sacks and threshing which was twenty cents; out of the remaining thirty cents he had to subtract the cost of putting in the crop and storing it and hauling it to market. The number of failures, especially amongst those who farmed land on shares, was notable. They were going broke on all sides. So it can be seen from the foregoing, that it was not all skittles and beer for the farmers.

I want to mention here, one of the most generous and best liked men, by all children and families in need; his name was "Jim Jacks," or "China Jim," the "Mustard King." [25]

Before the Flint-Bixby Co., began to lease their ground to the farmers there were immense crops of wild mustard growing on parts of it and when the renters began farming it there was a great deal of mustard which would always be found growing in the grain. This mustard, when the grain was being threshed, would be taken out by the cleaner that was running in conjunction with the separator. The farmers would throw the mustard seed away. "China Jim" began to gather this up. The farmer was glad to be rid of this seed and they gave it to him. He procured a number of large canvasses and with hand sieves, when the wind was blowing, he cleaned up the seed. He always got standing mustard where it had choked everything else out. This standing mustard he got cut by Chinese, with sickles, after which he would flail the seed out on a canvas.

"Jim" lived at what was always called "The Middle of the Lane," that is on the long straight lane, between San Juan and Hollister. He was employed by the Flint-Bixby Co., to poison squirrels and lived in a small house, and at times cooked for a few men that the company had employed there in the summer. He continued to collect mustard seed. He always drove a little one-horse cart, and in the front, at his feet, he carried a good-sized box in which he had candy in little bags, oranges and sweet cookies in small cartons. These he gave to the children on his trips to Hollister or San Juan. On the last day of school he would purchase a ten-pound bucket of the finest candy, and when asked what he was going to do with it, his reply was, "It is for the schoolmarm." I have known of him hiring a four-horse team and driver to take him to Hollister at which town he bought enough flour for a load, had it driven back to San Juan and distributed among the laboring men's families. On another occasion he bought three-hundred sacks of potatoes all of which he gave away. He also kept a few hens, the eggs he would take to the store and sell, receiving a credit slip for the sale.   These slips he would give to families whom he thought needed something out of the store.   No one ever knew how much money he had, unless it was his banker. I heard him say that he gave away all the interest on his money. When I was with a threshing outfit I would spread a sheet behind the cleaner for him.   Every year, a day or two before Thanksgiving, he would drive up the avenue and give my wife several packages of mincemeat, raisins, candies, and nuts.   To the children he would give fifty cents or a dollar each, and before he left he would get close to me and slip a dollar in my pocket and whisper, "You get a cup of beer."   He did not associate with the Chinese, except when he had them hired. After he got old he returned to China where he died.

There are but few of the early settlers that were residing at San Juan, when my parents moved there, now living.   I will endeavor to give a brief sketch of the few that still remain.

William Bingham, who resides on the old homestead in the San Juan Canyon, and who has enlarged his holdings by purchases, is one of the remaining settlers.   He has a very fine orchard growing in the canyon.   Mr. Bingham is a painter by trade, but dropped that calling for farming.   He now has an orchard of which he may well be proud.

Joseph and Adi Wilcox, son and daughter of Sylvester and Sarah Wilcox, are the remaining members of a large family that settled on the San Justo ranch in the early '50's.   They were residing in the valley when my parents came to San Juan. After the grant was sold to the Flint-Bixby-Hollister Co., the Wilcox family moved onto "The Alameda," outside of San Juan.   "Vess," as he was familiarly called, was a hard-working industrious, man, always busy at some task or another.   He was a carpenter, and followed that trade, conducting, on the side, a small dairy.   Mr. Wilcox was a man that you seldom saw in town, unless he had business to attend to there.   Joseph and Adi are following the same mode of life.   They have a nice home surrounded by a beautiful garden of trees and shrubs.

Neither of them have ever married. It is hard to tell who is the boss of that household, everything surrounding their home goes so quietly and smoothly.

The estate of the late John Breen, the adobe and a portion of the land, is still occupied by Mr. Breen's heirs. The Patrick and Edward J. Breen, estates are also in the possession of their heirs.

Jas. Stanley, who had a harness shop on the west side of Third street, between Mokelumne and Polk streets, was an Irishman. He was famous for work in his line and put up some of the most durable harness that could be procured in this state.

At his home, on the northwest corner of Tuolumne and Third streets, he erected a barn, and, buying two or three of the largest steers he could find, would feed them and fatten them solely for the purpose of showing the San Juanites how the Irish people in the "Auld Dart" handled cattle. The steers were fed everything that would fatten them. They were curried and brushed and blanketed. No thoroughbred race horse received better care. He would sell these animals for Christmas beef to butchers in San Francisco. Some of these steers would weigh nearly a ton. It is impossible to conceive that these fattened steers ever paid Stanley for the care that he bestowed upon them. It was an obsession upon the part of Stanley, who desired to show folks that when it came to raising cattle no one could surpass the Irish farmer.

Henry Beger carried on a boot and shoe store on the southwest corner of Mokelumne and Third streets.

Julius Brietbarth, who bought the southeast corner of Mariposa and Third streets, and conducted a boot and shoe business there, was known for the fine stock of goods that he carried in his line. Julius and his family lived in a part of this building. He was considered one of the best shoe and boot makers in this section of the state. It must be remembered that in the early days bootmaking was done by hand. As boots were generally worn, an artisan superior in this line usually gained wide recognition.   Julius was a very jovial man when away from the shop which gave rise to the rumor that sometimes things were not pleasant at home.   On one occasion, he took a shot at himself, but his suicidal attempt failed.   After accumulating quite a competence, he died, leaving all he possessed to his wife.

A noted character in his day, in San Juan, was John Anderson, commonly known as "The Tinsmith."   Anderson conducted a tinware store in the building formerly occupied by McMahon's merchandise store, on the southeast corner of Polk and Third street.   Like all early artisans, Anderson was not only a good tinsmith but he carried an excellent stock of goods as well.   He married a young woman who had formerly been in the employ of the Flint-Bixby Company as a cook.   It was rumored, from time to time, that he made life unpleasant for his wife.   After her death he married Mrs. Julius Brietbarth and moved his tinware store to the Brietbarth building previously mentioned.   A rumor became prevalent that all was not harmonious between Anderson and his second wife, owing to the fact that he admitted that he had to sleep in the tank-house connected with the residence.   However, their married life did not last long.   Mrs. Anderson, the second, in due time, passed away and, having no heirs, all her property, which amounted to considerable, passed to John Anderson.   John held on to his means tighter than the bark on a tree but, eventually, the Grim Reaper came along and carried John away.   Not knowing what to do with the property at his death, he bequeathed it all to the I. O. O. F. lodge of San Juan, of which he was a member.

So goes the weaving and spinning and cutting of the threads of life!

FLINT-BIXBY RANCH, CIRCA 1863

CHAPTER XXIX

Flint-Bixby Co.'s sheep enterprise in early days—Some of the Business houses between 1870 and 1880—In later years many changes in San Juan took place

WHEN the Flint-Bixby Co., drove across the plains their band of sheep it numbered upwards of four thousand head. Afterwards they sent east, to Vermont, and had shipped to them a French Merino buck which, at one time, when sheared, yielded forty-two pounds of wool. The rapidity with which the Flint-Bixby Co.'s herd multiplied may be imagined from the fact that it took from fifteen to twenty men to herd and look after the sheep. The company was the first to introduce into California the Spanish Merino sheep, which also were brought from Vermont. The climate, combined with the abundance of feed, caused the flocks to multiply rapidly. The company made it a point to hire none but Americans to shear their sheep, and it was not long ere it took sixteen shearers from fifty to sixty days to shear the flocks. The shearer would average close to one hundred sheared sheep a day, and the pay was six and a quarter cents for each sheep. In addition to this stipend the shearers received their board and lodging. They were always comfortably lodged, in a large bunk-house, which contained an enormous fireplace.

At times scab was prevalent amongst the sheep, and this disease was cured by driving the sheep into a long narrow vat, filled with boiled tobacco juice. The long trough, containing this juice, was constructed in such a fashion that the sheep had to swim through it from one end to the other, thus completely covering and soaking their fleeces with the tobacco juice. From the trough the sheep made their way up into a large pen which contained a slanting floor. This slant conducted the tobacco juice that ran off the sheeps' bodies back into the trough. The yearlings would be shorn in the fall.

The fame of their herd spread throughout the state, and they had a splendid trade in selling bucks to other flock owners who desired to improve the quality of their herds.

The Flint-Bixby Company were interested in various enterprises amongst which might be mentioned the Coast Line Stage Company, The Serra Benito Quicksilver Company, and the California Beet Sugar Company. [26]

Of the Flint family the following sons of Dr. Flint survive: Thomas Flint, Jr., who resides in Hollister and Richard Flint, who runs a dairy on the bank of the San Benito river, on the site of the old crossing, where the travelers in early days took the road leading to the San Joaquin Valley, via the Pacheco Pass. Benjamin Flint, now deceased, at the time of his death, owned a place on the south bank of the San Benito river on the west side of the grant. He was a son of Benjamin Flint, Sr.

Herewith are some of the business houses that were in San Juan between 1870 and 1880.

The brick building, now occupied by the Abbe Company, has sheltered many tenants. After the big fire in San Juan, that destroyed so much property on Third street, Dan Harris moved into this building, which the fire had not touched. In it he conducted a merchandise store. Eventually Dan turned over the business to his brother, Sam Harris. Sam, after conducting this business for a year or so, sold out to another partner and went to Santa Clara.

William Prescott, son of one of the earliest settlers in the San Juan Valley, still lives on the home place and is one of the most highly respected men in the valley. The elder Prescott was the first settler in the San Juan Valley that bored for and obtained artesian water. He also enjoyed the distinction of being the first farmer in the valley to set out an orchard. After his parents' death, William Prescott succeeded to the farm and has continued it ever since. He was, for a number of years, elected supervisor from the San Juan district. During his tenure of office he laid out and graded the San Benito county portion of the Chittenden road, which is one of the finest scenic roads leading into Watsonville. This route is far superior to any other. By laying out this Chittenden Pass road Mr. Prescott succeeded in eliminating the more torturous road by "The Rocks." Notwithstanding that his family is all grown up, "Bill" Prescott still sticks to the farm as rugged and hardy as ever.

One of the earliest settlers in the San Juan Valley was John Salthouse, who was farming there during the '50's. His nephew, the late John Welch, succeeded to the ownership of his farm. John Welch engaged in the butcher business, first in San Juan then in Hollister and eventually was elected county treasurer of San Benito county, which position he filled for years, until death removed him from the scene of his labors. Some of the Welch heirs still retain the Salthouse property.

Haydon Dowdy's heirs still retain possession of what was always known as the "Dowdy farm." His son, Frank Dowdy, now manages it. Haydon Dowdy, in his day, was the most conspicuous figure in San Benito county's politics. A strong and ardent Democrat, he was conceded to be, for years, the political boss of that county. A fine, honest and upright man was Haydon Dowdy. Mrs. Dowdy, still alive, resides in Hollister. The McKee family's farm, in San Juan Valley, is still managed by the heirs. Mrs. J. B. McKee unable to do her housework boards and lodges in Hollister.

The Andrew Abbe home on First street, San Juan, is still in the possession of the heirs.

One of the outstanding citizens of San Juan has always been P. E. G. Anzar, familiarly known to everyone in this section of the county as "Lupe" Anzar. Mr. Anzar was born in 1851, in the lower story of the Plaza Hotel building. In his youth he attended the San Juan schools; later on going to Santa Clara College, which he attended until the year 1871 when he went to Los Angeles and engaged in business there until 1876.   On his return from Los Angeles he married Mary Breen, widow of the late William Breen, with whom I attended school, in San Juan, in the early days.   Mrs. Anzar was born in the Plaza Hotel building, also.   She was the daughter of Angelo Zanetta.   When a girl she attended the sisters' convent at San Juan.

To Mr. and Mrs. Anzar have been born twelve children. This estimable couple celebrated their golden wedding about two years ago.   They are two of the most respected residents in San Benito county.   They are hale and hearty and enjoy the friendship of numerous friends and the loving kindness of their children; and, hand in hand, they are journeying through life.

Fernando Zanetta was born at Monterey in 1855, and soon after his birth his parents moved to San Juan.   Mr. Zanetta is still alive and enjoys life by sitting, on sunshiny days, on a bench alongside the Plaza livery stable, conducted by his brother "C. C." Zanetta.   If you want the history of San Juan told by a man thoroughly conversant with the history of that old-time town, wake up Fernando, sit down beside him and enjoy hearing stories of the past.   He is equal to Mark Regan when started.   He can tell you about the bull fights, the early overland stages, the early mission fathers and the various tragedies connected with San Juan.   He will regale you with many reminiscences that pour volubly from his lips.   One of the interesting incidents that he will relate is that he formerly drove the stage between Hollister and San Juan, and that one of the notable events connected with his career as a stage-driver was the day that he had the honor of taking Ike Mylar and his blushing bride over to Hollister on the day they were married.

One of the old residents of the valley was R. G. Norton, who lived a half mile from the east end of the lane.   Mr. Norton died some years ago but his heirs still occupy the place.

One of the old-timers well and favorably known throughout San Benito county until his death was William Burnett.
Mr. Burnett was, at one time, sheriff of San Benito county
and has ever since been credited as the only sheriff that ever
came out of office with any money. Jere Croxon, present
sheriff of the county, is married to one of Mr. Burnett's daughters. Burnett was a former stage driver and in early days ran
an independent stage line between Monterey and San Juan. In
after years he ran a stage from San Juan to New Idria. It was
Burnett's stage that passed a half hour earlier than usual going
towards New Idria on the day that Vasquez raided Paicines, and
killed three men. Burnett's farm is the first farm north of
the Middle of the Lane.

From 1872 to 1880, San Juan began to recover from the
many misfortunes that had overtaken her, the principal one
being the smallpox epidemic.

Business commenced to start up in the old town. Ike
Oderkirk established a fine blacksmith shop on the corner of
Second and Tuolumne streets. He had five men employed and
they were all kept busy.

Samuel Waldenburg, who had married Hulda, daughter
of E. A. Reynolds, started a general merchandise store located
on the west side of Second street, between Tuolumne and Jefferson streets. After leaving San Juan, Waldenburg conducted
the hotel at Firebaugh's ferry, on the San Joaquin river. This
he conducted with success for many years.

James Collins and John Silk ran a saloon located close
to Waldenburg's store.

On the northwest corner of Jefferson and Second streets,
Morris Sullivan built and conducted a general merchandise
store.

On the southwest corner of Jefferson and Second streets
George Pullen built and conducted a livery stable. Pullen,
at that time, was proprietor of the National Hotel.

The blacksmith and carriage shop, on the southwest corner of San Jose and Second streets, was conducted by E. W. Bowman and sons; Clarence, a blacksmith; William, a wheelwright and Walter, a painter. They also employed a smithy and helper to shoe horses. They branched out in the manufacture of wagons and buggies and also manufactured what was known, and popular, for years, among the farmers, as the "Bowman Gang Plow."

E. W. Bowman bought an outside lot on Fourth street and planted it to trees and cultivated this orchard until he retired from business. He finally sold a portion of this tract on which is located, at the present time, the San Juan water works. Clarence Bowman, after disposing of his business in San Juan, located near Corralitos, in Santa Cruz county, with his two brothers, William and Walter. All three engaged in the nursery business at that place, and their venture proved to be a very successful one. William Bowman has been in Sacramento for years. Clarence, after buying a farm in Pleasant Valley and raising a fine orchard, sold or traded it and moved away. His present residence is unknown to me. Walter is still at, or near, Corralitos. Mr. and Mrs. E. W. Bowman are deceased.

In July, 1870, Peter Breen, son of Patrick Breen, Sr., who was one of the Donner Party, was drowned in the Pajaro river, at the junction of that stream with the San Benito river, whilst swimming with some companions. He rode his horse into the deep water and it was thought the horse must have struck him in some manner. His body did not come to the surface. It was recovered by a diver. He was unmarried.

Between 1870 and 1880, at different times, the merchants of San Juan were as follows: Morris Sullivan, Joseph Bowie, F. A. Bacher, M. Gardella, B. Samit and M. Filloucheau.

William Cortney moved his store from Hollister into the building vacated by Joseph Bowie, on the northwest corner of Third and Washington streets. I well remember that store. I entered it, one day, for a purchase, and was waited on by Lizzie Cortney, the daughter of William Cortney. The girl had her jaws tied up and declared the affliction was mumps. Thinking that I had had all the diseases that a person was heir to I did not give it another thought. But, in a few days, I was laid up in bed with the mumps. I lived in a home, on the opposite side of the street, that had been occupied by William Prescott, he having lived there for a short time. In the bedroom I occupied some one had written with a pencil, "This is hell!" It seems the writer of the assertion had been confined there with the same disease. William Cortney later, sold his business in San Juan and located in Watsonville, on the east side of Main street, in a building that is now known as the "Kimona Shop." At that time he conducted it as a hotel.

Chas. Fowler, Jr., the son of Chas. Fowler who owned a farm in the Springfield district and ran a threshing machine for years, married Lizzie Cortney. Chas. Fowler, Jr., was the brother of Mrs. Jack Shea, of Brennan street, Watsonville.

The proprietor of the Plaza Hotel was A. Camours and the Plaza livery stable was conducted by A. Zanetta.

Dr. C. G. Cargill, who opened a well appointed drug store in connection with his practice, was appointed postmaster and was agent for Wells Fargo & Company's Express. Later, when the telephone came in vogue, he also had this office in connection with his other enterprises. [27]

The San Antonio Rancho had been partitioned and sold. Joseph Machado had bought the southeast lot of twelve hundred acres on which he had a dairy. The highway from San Juan to Salinas now runs through his tract.

Adjoining, on the west, was McAbee with another large acreage. On the west from this was a lot bought by T. McMahon. Of two of these lots one was sold to Phillip Dougherty, who was afterwards killed in the town of Hollister by being thrown from a wagon. Tom Conner bought the other lot. These lots lie one on each side of the "Rocks Road," between San Juan and Watsonville. [28]

Dan Wilson also owned land on both sides of the Watsonville road. This land extended to the road from San Juan to Sargent station. The line bounds the cemetery, on the west.

North from Wilson's place is the J. B. McKee farm; north of McKee's place John Mulligan resided. The E. J. Breen and Patrick Breen lands were farmed by renters, as was also a part of the San Justo Rancho.

Many people traded in San Juan, and, on Sunday, you would see them attending the churches, Protestant, and the old mission church.

The sisters of the convent could be seen marching their children, about fifty or sixty in number, to church. You could meet men from all around the country. Everyone was getting along nicely and appeared satisfied. Times continued this way for some time and then the town began to slump. First one would move away and then another.

The farmers on the San Antonio Rancho all moved away. The merchants left, the blacksmith shop proprietors and other tradesmen did likewise. The convent sisters took their little orphans and departed for Los Angeles. Some of the waifs were sent to the Santa Cruz Orphans' school, others were taken to the southern city. In the old mission yard, where you were wont to hear the merry prattle of children at play, could be seen cattle grazing. Petty thieves had ransacked the dormitories and rooms of the building where the orphan children had been maintained and had robbed the rooms of their furnishings and all paraphernalia that could be carried away. The two-story brick building that was used for a school room and dormitory, as well, the bricks and other material, were sold. Instead of the usual crowd that, formerly would be seen, on Sundays, coming along the corridor from the masses in the old mission, there were but a few left. The Protestant church, in the town, found it extremely difficult to secure a minister that could stay there on the living afforded. San Juan began to look almost like a ghost town on the Mother Lode.

This condition of affairs went on for a number of years, when, one day a stranger appeared in the town. He announced that he was looking for a place where cement material could be procured, and stated that he had been told to investigate the San Juan canyon. The business men, that were left, had a confab with him, and seemed pleased with the assurances given them. Ere long this stranger commenced to acquire the right-of-way for a railroad from Chittenden to the San Juan canyon, in which he also bought a plant site, and right-of-way for about two miles up the canyon. He brought a force of men to the mission town to work laying tracks, grading, and constructing bridges and culverts for the railroad. He also brought a large number of men to work in the San Juan canyon grading for the San Juan cement plant.

There was a large eating house built near the cement site and then business prospects to San Juan began to loom up again. People from all parts of the country began to come into the town looking for possible locations and other means of livelihood. Before long all the hitherto deserted buildings in the town were rented and carpenters commenced erecting new structures. All sorts of business enterprises, came to San Juan, restaurants, plumbing establishments, and a great many saloons.

One enterprising individual built a saloon on the right-of-way leading into the San Juan canyon. At this place he could supply the wayfarers coming and going with liquor refreshments. Real estate men commenced to take cognizance of the new state of affairs and property that hitherto went begging now commenced to change hands.

Mark Regan, the veteran jehu reaped a rich harvest as his stage plied between Sargent station and the old mission town; (or, as Mark always described it, "the mother of all the missions,") loaded with passengers.

Soon work on the cement plant commenced, and a large force of men were. engaged in pouring cement and laying the foundations.

Geo. Tremaine, who owned a fine orchard in San Juan canyon, divided his holdings up into lots, many of which were sold.

One day the cement plant's train of cars came into the old mission town and San Juan had a railroad at last. The first freight agent appointed on the new railroad was Mark Regan. He was freight agent, conductor and brakeman and on all the passes that he issued he signed himself superintendent of the San Juan-Portland Cement Co.'s Railroad. He had a bus at the little station and his driver would take you to any part of the town.

Soon after the railroad was completed, from Chittenden to the cement plant site, the machinery for the plant began to arrive. The place became a beehive of industry. Some of the pieces of machinery used in the plant were so long that they were stretched on top of from two to three flat cars. Some of the machinery weighed tons, in fact, all the machinery for the plant was very heavy. This machinery and steel to be used in the plant kept constantly arriving and when stretched out on the ground covered fully two or three acres of the plant's holdings.

Then something happened! The men were laid off. They hung around for a while. Surely this big enterprise could not stop now. Over half a million dollars were invested in the enterprise. But, everything connected with it stopped. The men who had thus far managed the project went away, and everything connected with the undertaking was left in a state of confusion.

The machinery was left on the ground to rust, so was the locomotive, standing idly by, and thus it remained until some of the creditors came to San Juan and shipped a large portion of the machinery and other paraphernalia away. San Juan was left to sink into the slough of despondency, again.

After a while—some time after—a new company was formed who took over the holdings of the former promoters and shipped in there the necessary machinery and commenced work without any preliminary fussing or blowing.

While this cement industry has helped San Juan, in a way, it has not been what the people had been led to expect as regards the great benefit which they would derive from it.

Poor old San Juan Bautista! You have seen many happy and many despondent days. You have been knocked down and dragged out, kicked, and cuffed, and almost took the count; but, still you are in the ring. San Juan has had many handicaps. She never could expand on account of the large landownings in her immediate vicinity. Imagine the result had Col. Hollister retained the west half of the San Juan Valley in place of the east half.

Concluding these memoirs, I feel that I have not done justice to the memory of those early pioneers, or their descendants, of Old San Juan Bautista.

They stand out clearly in my mind as the best there is in humanity.

True friendship is a rare gem; I found it in that old mission town.

Looking backward, the ever-changing kaleidoscope of life, brings recollections of some very pleasant memories, as well as some sad ones.

It is hard to realize the great changes that have taken place in the old home town; for San Juan Bautista will always be "home town" to me.

FAREWELL

Notes and References

1. "No grade," as used here, appears to mean "no improved road."

2. Secularization was already in effect at the Mission San Juan Bautista in 1839, when the Rancho San Justo was granted to General Jose Castro by Mexican Governor Juan B. Alvarado.

3. In 1873, the rapidly growing new town of Hollister was host to the fifty teachers attending the Monterey County teachers' institute arranged by Superintendent of Schools Samuel M. Shearer.

4. Though still a good load for a pack animal, three flasks of quicksilver would have weighed about 125 pounds less than the amount indicated.

5. Francisco Perez Pacheco had bought the San Justo grant from General Castro, the grantee. Flint, Bixby & Co., whose members were Benjamin Flint, Dr. Thomas Flint, and Llewellyn Bixby, purchased the property on October 2, 1855, with the understanding that Col. W. W. Hollister would eventually acquire an undivided half interest in the ranch. This understanding became an accomplished fact two-and-a-half years later, when Mrs. Lucy A. Brown completed payment on behalf of her brother.

6. Partition of the Rancho San Justo on November 30, 1861, gave Col. Hollister the larger eastern portion, and Flint, Bixby & Co. the portion closer to San Juan and more accessible to the county seat at Monterey and to the shipping facilities at Alviso.

7. Llewellyn Bixby's young brother was named Solomon.

8. Jacob Watson was known as the first settler on the eastern portion of the San Justo grant, where he had established his home in 1854. On October 27, 1855, settlers instrumental in organizing a mass meeting in San Juan to protest Pacheco's sale of the grant to Flint, Bixby & Co. included Joseph R. Beals (p. 149), T. R. Davidson, H. S. Hawver, H. S. Jones, William Jordan, and H. H. Smith, according to their communication published in the *San Jose Telegraph* of November 6, 1855. Still other names appearing on an early map of the grant (along with those of Col. Hollister and the Wilcox brothers) are Ball, Barker, and Ch. Rose.

9. The Hon. E. C. Tully of Bitterwater was assemblyman for Monterey County at the time of the county division in the 20th session of the State Legislature in 1874. Later he represented San Benito County in the 28th session. The Hon. John H. Matthews served in the 24th, 25th, 27th, and 30th sessions.

10. The vaquero mentioned was Refugio Echevarria. (See also p. 82.) Difficulties with spelling or pronunciation of names and other words from the area's Spanish and Mexican background and from the influx of settlers from various parts of the world were not unusual in early San Juan. The French surname "Taix" (pp. 135 and 174) quickly became a homonym of "tax," and the familiar "tocalote" (the commonly used designation of the Napa thistle) may have undergone a similar modification that caused it to appear as the Italianate "Tuccoletta" (p. 55) remembered by Isaac Mylar.

11. Three successive school buildings on First Street were used in the hundred years beginning with the late 1860's and ending with the late 1960's.

12. Major Emanuel McMichael, a South Carolinian, a forty-niner, and an enthusiastic lifelong Democrat, served as a commissioner to determine disputed land-grant boundaries, and afterward as postmaster at San Juan in the first administration of President Cleveland. Prior to the latter appointment, he had suffered heavy losses in the great drought of 1863-64 and again in the early 1870's, when he had tried unsuccessfully to develop the Cerro Bonito quicksilver mines located south of Hollister. When he died at "four score and four years," according to a newspaper dispatch of March 2, 1893, "business was entirely suspended" in San Juan on the day of the funeral. His daughter's appointment to the post-office position came in the second Cleveland administration shortly after her father's death.

The Hon. Thomas Flint, Jr., represented Monterey and San Benito counties in the State Senate for sixteen years beginning in 1889, and served as President pro tem of that body for the last ten of those years.

13. The Masonic building at Second and Mokelumne was built in 1868 and dedicated on June 24, 1869.

14. The earliest route of El Camino Real southward across the Gabilans from Mission San Juan Bautista began its ascent in the San Juan Canyon, where a well-defined trace may still be seen.

15. The "three other young fellows" were uncles of the young Isaac Mylar, according to biographies published in *A Memorial and Biographical History of the Coast Counties of Central California* (Barrows and Ingersoll, eds., 1893).

16. For the location of a route antedating all three roads remembered by the author, see note for p. 85.

17. "Roche" is the spelling used in the regional history already cited and in a newspaper obituary of August, 1898.

Marcellus and Jotham Bixby moved to Southern California after Flint, Bixby & Co. purchased the Rancho Los Cerritos in Los Angeles County in 1866. There, they were joined by their cousin, John W. Bixby, who was young, unmarried, and "newly come from Maine," according to Sarah Bixby Smith's *Adobe Days*.

18. In this chapter, "Overland" should be read "Coast Line" except in one instance on p. 130 ("drivers graduated from the old Overland Stage Company"). Flint, Bixby & Co. acquired the Coast Line Stage Co. in 1868 from Llewellyn Bixby's brother-in-law, William E. Lovett (p. 114), who had been operating the line for about two years.

19. Official rainfall figures announced by the United States Signal Service for San Francisco show 49.27 inches in 1861-62, and 10.08 inches in 1863-64. For the later dry year of 1876-77 (p. 167), the figure is 9.87 inches. Records kept at the Rancho San Justo for the years 1880-1912 indicate that maximum annual rainfall during that period was 36.48 inches in 1889-90, the minimum 9.28 inches in 1897-98.

20. In 1868 the San Justo Homestead Association was the buyer, and Col. Hollister the seller, in a $370,000 transaction. (See also notes for pp. 39 and 40).

21. The naming of the town of Hollister has been ascribed, always in a story similar to this one, to at least two other men. The minutes of the San Justo Homestead Association merely record the decision.

The site of the Hollister home—on Fourth Street between Monterey and West—has been marked by a commemorative plaque since 1965.

22. Having retired briefly to his private law practice at the end of the appointive term mentioned, Judge Breen later served in the Assembly during the 22nd session and as Superior Judge of San Benito County in 1880-97. He was succeeded in the later office by the Hon. Maurice T. Dooling (p. 81), who had also served for a single session (the 26th) in the Assembly.

23. The Hon. Thomas Beck was senator for Monterey and Santa Cruz counties during the period of turmoil over the division of the former county in 1871-75. In 1875-79 Dr. Thomas Flint represented Monterey, San Benito, and Santa Cruz counties.

24. A reprint of a fictionalized account of events referred to in this chapter, *The Sanchez Treasure,* by Edward White, has recently been issued with addenda by the Pajaro Valley Historical Association. The original was serialized in an unidentified newspaper in 1919.

25. The obvious nickname "Jim Jack" (not "Jacks") was customarily spoken as if it were a single word with the accent on the first syllable, as in "racetrack" or "smokestack."

26. The indicated mining enterprise was called the Cerro Bonito. (See note for p. 72.)

27. Dr. Charles G. Cargill served as assemblyman in the 29th, 31st, and 33rd sessions. Completing the roster of nineteenth century San Benito County members of the Assembly, were—in addition to those mentioned in the notes for pp. 44 and 160—the Hon. George M. Roberts of the 21st session, the Hon. J. J. Harris of the 23rd session, and the Hon. C. F. Rubell of the 32nd. Seven of the eight were members of the Democratic party, Dr. Cargill being the one Republican. In the same period of (1874-1900), the area was represented in the State Senate by three out-of-county Democrats for a total of seven years, by an out-of-county adherent of the short-lived Workingmen's party for four years, and by two San Juan Republicans for sixteen years. (See notes for pp. 72 and 164.)

28. An account of ranch life along the Rocks Road "from 1894 till 1904" is included in *The Life and Times of Philip Dougherty,* 1828-1903, privately printed and distributed by his son, Paul Daugherty, in 1865.

Index

Abbe, Andrew - 43, 55, 67, 69, 70, 82, 187
Abbe, Charles - 69
Abbe, Clara - 55
Abbe Company - 61, 186
Abbe, Frank - 69, 70
Abbe, Fred - 69, 70
Abbe, George - 69, 70
Alameda County - 15
Alameda, The - 44, 48, 49, 58, 59, 83, 168, 181
Alisal - 16
Allyn, Wm. - 14
Alta California - 9
Amesti Ranch - 108
Anderson, John (The Tinsmith) - 183
Anderson, Mrs. - 183
Anzar, Anatol - 111
Anzar Family - 131
Anzar, Mrs. J. - 111
Anzar, Joseph - 20
Anzar, Juan - 111
Anzar, P.E.G. (Lupe) - 111, 112, 131, 143, 187 -188
Arguello, Santiago - 20
Arnold, Bill - 75
Aromas - 161
Aromas Valley - 157
Azul, Madame - 51

Bacher, F.A. - 190
Baker, Albion - 96, 145
Barker, Andrew - 56, 69, 75, 76
Beals, Joe - 149
Bean, Josh - 120
Beck, Fred - 173
Beck, Thomas - 164
Beger, Henry - 182
Bell, Tom - 37
Bernal, Mrs. Jesus - 61
Beuttler, Albert - 173
Beuttler, Annie - 173
Beuttler, George - 173
Beuttler, Jake - 173
Bickmore, Mrs. Thomas - 34, 44
Bigley, John - 61, 67, 71

Bingham, William - 181
Bird Creek - 101, 169
Birmingham, Alec - 64
Birmingham, John - 64, 116
Bixby, John - 126
Bixby, Llewllyn - 39, 41, 114
Bixby, Marselle - 126
Black, Frank - 66
Black, Jim - 160
Blair, Mr. - 115
Bolado, Joaquin - 165
Booth, Gov. Newton - 159
Borondo - 66, 81
Borica, Governor - 9
Bowie, "Aunt Eliza" - 63
Bowie Brothers - 62
Bowie, Joe - 63, 190
Bowman, Clarence - 64, 66, 190
Bowman, E. W. - 190
Bowman, Walter - 190
Bowman, William - 190
Brandon, Mr. - 43
Breen, Edward - 55, 182, 192
Breen Family - 54, 136
Breen's Grove - 126
Breen, Judge James F. - 35, 71, 115, 160
Breen, John -16, 125, 140, 159, 182
Breen, Margaret - 115
Breen, Mary - 188
Breen, Patrick - 182, 192
Breen, Patrick, Sr. - 51, 81, 27, 55, 112, 125, 136, 190
Breen, Peter - 190
Breen, Samuel - 51, 55, 115
Breen, William - 112, 136, 188
Breen, Mrs. William - 112
Brietbarth, Julius - 182
Brietbarth, Mrs. Julius - 183
Brietbarth Shoe Store - 62
Briggs, N. C. - 81, 159
Brotherton, R. H. - 79, 80, 81
Brown, J. M. (Baldy) - 165
Brown, John - 114
Brown & Williamson (Eureka Canyon Saw Mill) - 109

Brummett, Caleb - 65
Brummett, Harwell - 66
Bryerly & Clevenger
    (Central Californian Newspaper) - 164
Buckley, William - 127, 130
Buenaventura Family - 81
Bullier, Leon - 62-77
Burnett, Bill - 71, 90, 189
Burns, Miss - 120
Butron, Manuel - 58
Byrd, Bill - 63
Byrd, James - 63

Cabrillo - 9
Calaveras Co. - 61
Caldwell - 15
California Beet Sugar Company - 186
Camours, A. - 191
Campbell, Dr. & Mrs. - 34
Campbell, Mr. - 44
Canfield Family - 120
Canfield, Fanny - 70
Canfield, Lucy - 80
Cantua Canyon - 95
Cargill, Dr. C. G. - 55, 114, 191
Carlos, Pedro - 81
Carlton - 66
Carneros Section - 157, 161
Carr, Jesse D. - 86
Carreaga Family - 79
Carreaga, Juan - 81, 82
Carreaga, Ramon - 81, 82
Carson, Nevada - 16
Castro Family - 51, 54
Castro, General - 27, 136
Castro, Juan B. - 157
Castroville - 31, 32, 157, 161
Celis, Juan - 20
Cement Plant - 85
Cemetery - 22
Chalmers, Alex - 44
Chalmers, George - 44, 66, 116
Chatlaine, Mr. - 55
Chavez, Luis - 48,
    79, 83, 84, 90, 91, 93, 94, 95
Cheverria, Ramon - 82
Cheverria, Refugio - 65
China Jim - 178, 180
Chittenden Pass - 120, 187
Cholame Canyon - 95
Clark, Sam - 70
Clark, Tom - 33, 64, 129
Clay, Henry - 32
Clay, Tom - 32
Closa, Father Valentin - 25
Coalinga - 95, 144
Coastline Stage Company - 186

Collins, James T. - 120, 147, 149, 189
Columbia, Tuolumne County - 15
Comfort, John - 135
Comfort & Zanetta - 54
Conner, Tom - 192
Connolly, Mr. & Mrs. - 92
Cooper, Mr. - 28
Corralitos, Santa Cruz County
    44, 84, 100, 109, 169
Cortez - 11
Cortney, Lizzie - 191
Cortney, William - 190, 191
Cot, Antonio - 20
Crane, George W. (Judge) - 115, 176
Craw Family - 120
Cremony, J. C. (Major) - 118, 119
Crooks, Cassius - 44
Crooks, Family - 43, 44
Crooks, N. - 145
Crooks, Mr. - 43
Croxon, Jere - 189
Cullumber, John - 44
Cullumber, Martha - 34, 44
Cullumber, Sam - 44

Daley, Charles - 101, 123
Daley, Henry - 123
Daley, Hugh - 101, 123
Daley, James - 123
Daley, Sr. - 123
Danti, Friar - 9
Davidson, Leland - 93, 94
DeBard, Frank - 56
DeHart, William - 107
Dickinson, John H. - 53
Dolleguy, Mr. - 56
Donner Party - 27, 64, 136, 190
Dooling, Hon. M. T. (Judge) - 81
Dougherty, Phillip - 191
Dowdy, Elmer - 170
Dowdy, Haydon - 159, 169, 187
Dowdy, Frank - 120, 139, 187
DuBois, Cy - 43
Dunbarton - 175
Durin, Monsieur - 54, 76

Edmondson Family - 72, 73
El Camino Real (The King's Highway)
    15, 47, 121, 127
Emmett - 119
Emmons, James - 71

Fair, Sen. James - 14
Ferguson, Mary - 25
Fernando VII - 10
Filousheau, Mr. - 52, 53, 62, 190
Flint, Ben - 39, 43, 122, 148, 186

200

Flint- Bixby Co. - 40, 41, 49,
  83, 86, 127, 151, 168, 180, 181,
  183, 185, 186
Flint, Richard - 63, 186
Flint, Dr. Thomas - 39, 63,
  71, 86, 113, 139, 160, 114
Flint Home - 123
Flint, Hon. Thomas Jr. - 72, 186
Font, Capt. - 10
Ford, Charles Co. - 65
Forney, John - 52
Foster, Captain - 16
Foster, John - 20
Fowler, Charles Jr. - 191
Fowler, Charles Sr. - 191
Francis, Mr. Bob (Family) - 42, 43
Franciscans - 9
Freiermuth, Harry - 105
Freiermuth, P. J. - 105
Fremont's Peak - 157
French, Miss - 29
Friedlander & Co. - 141
Fulgium, Frank - 129

Gabilan Range - 39, 111, 121
Gardella, Felipe - 36, 61, 62
Gardella, M. - 190
Gaster, John - 74, 116, 129
Gates & Baptist - 164
German, Chino - 57
German, Felipe - 57
German, Pablo - 57
Giacoma, Mr. - 174
Gillis, Steve - 15
Gilman, Joe C. - 113
Gilroy - 9, 37, 88, 113, 144, 154, 155
Gonzales, Juan - 90, 91
Goodrich, Charles - 70, 145
Graham, Arthur - 70, 168
Gregory - 115
Griffin - 63, 131
Guerra, Jose de la - 10

Hagen, Mr. - 153
Haley, Mr. - 92
Hall, Mr. - 63, 66
Hames, Benjamin - 100
Hanna and Furlong
  (Bodfish Canyon Sawmill) - 109
Harris, Alfred - 29
Harris, Amelia - 29
Harris, Byrd -83
Harris, Dan - 29, 36, 37, 56,
  61, 65, 129, 186
Harris, Sam - 62, 186
Harris, Simeon - 29
Harris, Wm. B. - 27, 85

Hart, Dr. - 112, 113
Hawkins, Thomas - 36, 152, 159
Hayes, H. M. - 159
Hebron, Hon. J. R. - 158
Hebbron's Lake - 121
Hernandez, southern San Benito
  County - 146
Hernandez, Rafael - 83, 145, 146
Heritage, Joe - 116
Hickey, Connor - 49, 71
Hinds, Mr. -165
Hodgdon, Roscoe - 69, 73
Hodges, Charles - 33
Hodges, Jim - 153
Hodges, Fielding - 33, 66, 143
Hodges, Samuel - 33
Hodges, Wm. - 33
Hollenbeck Family - 64
Hollister - 43, 64, 123,
  125, 151, 154, 155, 156, 158,
  159, 161, 162, 164, 165,
Hollister Bee - 163
Hollister, Colonel - 100, 101, 108,
  113, 126, 151, 153, 195
Hollister Enterprise - 163
Hollister Free Lance - 163
Hollister, Mr. (Colonel) - 19, 40
Hollister, W. W. - (Colonel) - 39
Holliwell, Benjamin - 122
Hopper, John (Hooper) - 52, 134
Hubbard, W. G. - 70, 72, 73, 137
Hunt, John - 71, 108, 109

Indian Corners - 123
Ingels, Tom - 119
I. O. O. F. Lodge - 183

Jacks, Jim ("China Jim-Jack"
  and "Mustard King") - 178-181
Jackson, Helen Hunt - 136
James, Evans -"Johnny Bull" -
  145 - 146
Jerbet, Victor - 79
Johnny Bull - 145
Johnny, Uncle - 44
Johnson, Dr. - 114
Jones, A. D. "San Juan Echo" - 164
Jordan, Amanda - 120
Jordan, Frank - 120
Jordan, John - 27, 120
Jordan, John Jr. - 120
Judd, Hugh - 108

Kelly - 89
Kemp Family - 64
Kemp, Fred - 64, 75, 76, 77
Kemp, Fred Jr. - 77
Kemp Saloon - 76, 77, 118, 177

Kennedy, Annie (Mrs. McConnell) - 95

Ladd, Len - 164-165
Larios, Don Manuel - 22, 81, 121
Lasuen, President - 9
Lavagnino's - 61
Laveaga, D. E.
 (Quien Sabe Rancho) - 133
Lawn, Dr. A. R. - 84
Lee, Julius - 115
Levia, Adone - 90-91
Lincoln, Abraham - 144
Linscott, James A.
 (Supervisor Santa Cruz Co.) - 84
Livermore Pass - 15
Los Angeles - 16, 94, 111
Los Angeles Co. - 90
Lovett, W. E. - 72, 114
Lowe, Frederick - 118
Lynch, Bill - 120
Lynch, Judge - 47
Lynch, Nancy - 120
Lynch, Susie - 120

Machado, Joseph - 191
Magner, Thomas - 79
Mankins, Pete - 108
Martin, Rev. Azariah - 28
Martinelli, Stephen - 138
Mathews, John - 34
 (Uncle Johnny - 44)
Mathews, Dr. Robert - 33, 44, 120
Mathews, Sam - 34
McAbee - 191
Mc Connell, George W.
 (Assessor of San Benito Co.) - 95-145
McCray, Frank P. - 160
McDougall, Dr. F. A. - 111
Mc Garvey, Vick - 70, 75, 76
Mc Gonigle, John - 163
Mc Ilroy, Capt. - 119
Mc Inerny, Jimmy - 130
McKee, J. B. - 81, 192
McKee, Mrs. J. B. - 187
Mc Kinley, James - 20
Mc Knight, T. J. - 64, 115
Mc Mahon, Kate - 71
Mc Mahon, James Sr.
 35, 63, 71, 74, 79, 131
Mc Mahon, Tom - 35, 159, 174, 191
Mc Mahon's Store - 63, 131, 174, 183
Mc Michael, Annie - 72
Mc Michael, Major - 72
Miller, Bloomfield Ranch - 89
Miller, Henry - 140
Miller, James - 63, 116
Miller, John - 62

Missing Link - 164 (newspaper)
Mitchell, Charles - 71, 145
Mondregon - 82
Monroe, Mrs. R. D. - 167
Monterey County - 9, 47,
 53, 90, 157, 158, 160, 161, 162
Montgomery, Edward - 154
Montgomery House (Hotel) - 154
Moore - 72
Moore, Abner - 139
Moore Family - 120
Moore, George - 43
Moore, Mrs. Sam - 94
Morales - (Musician) - 82
Morelas - (Surgeon) - 10
Morina - 90-91
Morris, H. C. - 160
Morse, Harry
 (Sheriff of Alameda) - 90
Mossup, George - 34
Mossup, L. E. - 34
Mossup, Mrs. L. E. - 33
Mossup, Victor - 34
Mount Madonna - 109-113
Mulligan, John - 192
Murietta, Joaquin - 48, 90-95
Murray, Henry - 91
Mustard King - 178-181
Mylar, Bob - 108, 123
Mylar, Cora - 167
Mylar, Earl - 167
Mylar, Edna - 167
Mylar, Enoch - 140
Mylar, Ike - 108, 188
Mylar, Isaac L. - Foreward
Mylar, Oscar - 167

Nagel, Jack - 73
National Hotel - 129, 147, 189
Natividad - 16, 121
New Almaden Quick Silver Mines
 63, 176
New Idria - 36-37, 40, 90, 118-119,
 129, 139-142, 155, 189
Nidever, Mrs. - 71
Nigger Bill - 142
Norton, R. G. - 188

Oakland - 14
Oderkirk, Mike - 189
Odom Family - 120
Odom, Mr. - 120
O'Flynn, Mrs. - 136
O'Neil, Charles - 75
Orton, Robert - 108
Overland Stage - 127, 135-137
Owens, J. A. - 154

Pacheco, Don - 39, 151
Pacheco Pass - 39, 80, 186
Pacheco Ranch - 141
Pacific Coast, The Newspaper - 163
Page, Mrs. - 89
Paicines - 90, 159-162, 189
Pajaro River - 107-108, 144, 174-175
Pajaro Valley
  63, 108, 157, 161-162, 168
Palmtag, Uncle Chris - 138
Palmtag Vineyard
  (Bird Creek Road) - 52
Palmtag, William - 53, 138
Panoche 95-118
Panoche Valley - 144
Pardino - 10
Pathfinder, The - 8
Peckham, (Attorney) - 115
Pennypacker, Mr. - 43
Pescadero Creek - 107, 125
Pescadero Canyon - 108
Pico, Andreas - 20
Pico, Governor - 16, 20-21
Pierce, E. A. - 70
Pilar, Madame - 65
Piratsky, James G. - Foreward, 69
Placerville - 13
Plaza Hotel - 27, 129
Pleasant, Mammy - 37
Pleasant Valley - 95, 167
Pomeroy, Mark - 159-160
Pratolongo, Mr. - 36, 56
Prescott, William Sr.
  120, 186-187, 191
Prescott, W. S. - 120, 187
Procopio - 90
Pullen, Frank - 147-148
Pullen, George - 147-148, 189
Pullman, George - 173

Quinn - 85
Quinn Canyon - 85

Rafferty, Lieut. - 119
Raggio's Canyon - 123
Raggio, Louis Jr. - 95
Raggio, Louis Sr. - 57-58, 85, 123
Rancho San Antonio - 22
Rector Bros. -167
Redford, George - 92, 94
Regan, Mark - 64, 173, 188, 193, 194
Reid, Hugo - 20
Reynolds, E. A. - 64, 129, 130, 189
Rider - 109
Roache, James H. - 115, 126, 146, 176
Rocks, The - 22, 175
Rocks Road - 22, 27-28, 192
Rolls, Bob -111
Rosas, Ambrosio - 124 (Rozas)
Ross, Annie - 57

Ross, Benjamin F. - 159
Ross, Cal - 57
Ross, Frank - 27, 52-53, 120
Rowls, Bob - 65
Roza Family - 62
Rozas Family Saloon - 62
Rupe, John - 120
Rupe, Mrs. - 33
Rupe, Tile - 33
Russell, George - 130
Russell and Reynolds - 145
Saint John The Baptist - 10
Saint John's Day - 10, 131, 133
Sal, Lt. - 9
Salinas - 157, 160-161
Salinas Index - 29
Salinas Plains - 15
Salthouse, John - 120, 187
Samit, B. - 190
San Antonio Rancho - 22, 191-192
San Benito - 118, 159
San Benito River
  9, 40, 140-141, 144, 148, 186
San Benito Valley - 9
San Buena Ventura Mission - 20
San Carlos - 10
Sanchez, Gregorio - 52, 56, 70, 115
Sanchez, Mrs. Gregorio - 115
Sanchez Land Grant - 81
Sanchez, Senor - 174, 175, 176
San Diego Mission - 20, 25
San Fernando Mission - 20
Sanford, Dr. - 115, 176
Sanford, Fidella - 115
Sanford, Mrs. - 115
San Gabriel Mission - 20
San Jose Mission - 15
San Juan Canyon - 39, 49,
  84-85, 123, 139, 181, 193-194
San Juan Capistrano - 10, 20
San Juan Cement Co. Plant - 85, 193
San Juan Creek - 140, 149
San Juan Echo - 164
San Juan Enterprise - 164
San Juan "Lane"
  40-41, 113, 139, 180, 188-189
San Juan Mission Church - 19, 150
San Juan Mission News - 164
San Juan Valley - 24, 97, 103,
  109, 118, 120, 146, 169, 170, 195
San Justo Rancho - 39, 40, 43, 44,
  55, 81, 126, 151, 181, 192
San Justo Homestead
  Association, Inc. - 151
San Luis Rey Mission - 20
Santa Ana District - 165
Santa Ana Valley - 41, 141
Santa Clara - 10, 90, 104
Santa Clara Mission 15, 47

Sargent, Jim - 63
Sargent Station (Sargent's)
139-140, 155, 173-174, 193
School House - 22
Sebastopol Hotel - 131, 135
Serra Bonito Quicksilver Co. - 186
Serra, Father Junipero - 9
Shakelford, Dick - 165
Shaw, George Bernard - 163
Shaw, Mr., (Hollister Advance) - 163
Shaw Flat (Tuolumne County) - 14
Shea, Mrs. Jack - 191
Shearer, Samuel - 28, 29, 30
Shelland, Mary Jane - 112-113
Sherwood, Ernie (Shorty) - 65
Sherwood, Mrs. Ernest - 167
Sherwood, Mr. & Mrs. Charles - 65
Silk, John - 73, 189
Simmons, Clara - 114
Simmons, Dr. - 64, 114
Simmons, Elmer - 114
Sinclair, Pruett - 109
Smith, Miss Leigh Margaret - 125
Smith, Lewis - 91, 94
Smith, James - 123
Smith, Wesley - 63
Snyder, A. - 90, 92, 93, 94
Soap Lake - 141
Soberanos - 21
Soledad - 121
Soledad Mission - 47
Sonora - 14
Soto - 90
Soto, Benino - 124
Spitts, Florence - 40, 42
Stanley, James - 65, 182
Stingley, William - 84, 107
Stramner Family - 122
Stramner, Lucy - 122
Stramner, Sinai - 122
Strode, Mr. - 75
Studebaker - 13
Sullivan, Morris - 71, 189, 190

Taix, A. - 174
Taix, Tony - 135
Table Mountain - 14
Taylor, Bart - 57, 85
Taylor, Capt. - 85
Tejon Pass - 47
Temple, John - 21
Thomas - 108
Thomas, J. W.
    "Missing Link" newspaper - 164
Thorne, Elizabeth Adelia - 167
Thorne, William - 43
Three Finger Jack - 48
Tremaine, George - 194
Tres Pinos - 118, 145, 155, 165
Tuccoletta Hall - 55
Tuttle, Mrs. M. B. - 119
Twain, Mark - 15

Twitchell, Jasper - 54, 85, 137
Twitchell, Joshua - 84, 86, 134
Twitchell, Lorenzo - 84
Twitchell, Silas - 107

Ubach, Padre - 24
Uzuruth, John - 91

Vacca, Pablo - 112
Vache, Adolphe - 54
Vache, Theophile - 52-54
Vallecitos, Calaveras County - 13-14
Vasquez, Tiburcio
    48, 89-90, 92-93, 94-95, 189
Viader, Padre - 10

Waldenberg, Hulda - 189
Waldenberg, Samuel - 189
Waterfront, (Fourth St.) - 48, 51
Watson, Dave - 44, 160
Watson, Henry - 44
Watson, Steve - 44
Watsonville - 63, 108, 113-114, 148
Webb - 115
Welch, Jack - 120
Welch, John - 187
Wells Fargo and Company
    Express - 191
Wentworth, C. W. - 154
West Coast Alliance Newspaper - 163
Western Hotel (Hollister) - 167
Westfall, Dr. - 114
White & De Hart - (White Ranch)-109
Whitney, John - 116
Whitton, Jess - 159
Wiggins, William "Dr." - 176-177
Wilcox, Adi - 83, 181
Wilcox, Benjamin - 43, 44, 45, 167
Wilcox, Edward - 45
Wilcox, Joseph - 45, 56, 83, 181
Wilcox, Mary - 167
Wilcox, Sarah - 181
Wilcox, Sylvester (Vess) 45, 83, 181
Williamson, Bill - 108
Williamson, Nels - 108
Wilson, Dan - 115, 192
Wilson, Woodrow - 170
Winn, W. B. - 69
Wise & Co. - 141
Wise, Mr. -54
Woods, A. C. - 140
Woods, Billy - 145
Woods, Hy - 57, 140
Woods, John - 140
Woodside & Gregory (Attorneys) - 115
Woodworth, Lon - 134
Workman, John - 20

Zanetta, Angelo - 55, 70,
    112, 131, 134-135, 188, 191
Zanetta, Ernest (C. C.) - 55,
    64, 116, 188
Zanetta, Fernando - 143, 188